"MORE THAN AN AMERICAN"

"From Immigration, Assimilation, English-Only, to Recycled Empires, and Reflections of the Racist Moon"

An Intimate Study

BY

Young-jim-fong Larriva

Alamosa, Colorado

www.bookstandpublishing.com

Published by
Bookstand Publishing
Morgan Hill, CA 95037
3148_1

ISBN 978-1-58909-739-1

Printed in the United States of America

~ACKNOWLEDGEMENTS~

Dedicated to my beloved sister Alicia
who adopted me into her household...otherwise I
might still be sleeping on cardboard boxes
and eating shadow food.

§ Mahalo to: Adams State College
for allowing me to "nest"in its library while
I attended to this project, and for letting me play in the
Art Department for the last several years.

Gracias to: Sarah J. Hudelson (Arizona State University)
for her encouragement to write.

The opinions in this book solely belong to the author.

At this time I wish to express the fondness I have for
the following dear people:

Young James Christian
Young John Micah
Jessica Rhema-Joy
Dave Roepke
Jade Pearl
La Joya
Persephone
and
Arigato to Ben and Alice Fujii

Preface

I began this study three years ago after moving back to the U.S. mainland. Since I had been living in Hawaii for the last thirty years, I felt quite ignorant of what had occurred historically in the U.S. during that time. Believe it or not, I had not heard much of the grape boycotts by César Chávez nor of the wars in El Salvador, Honduras, and Guatemala. Balmy Hawaii can have such a numbing effect on you; the waves can wash, rinse, and erase difficult news before it ever gets to you.

In March of 2007, I began to investigate the topic of immigration for myself because I began to see that many undocumented workers were being terrorized (families being separated, others rounded up and being treated like cattle, others even killed like the young man in Shenandoah, Pennsylvania) as ignorant (not knowing) people in power made overly quick judgments about a people merely looking for bread. I began to care deeply about this issue because I could literally hear twelve million people hiding in the darkest shadows crying out, **"No one deserves to live stuck in a silent scream."** I also had an "extra" interest in all this because as a small boy I had grown up on the U.S.-Mexican border towns of Tijuana, Mexicali, and Nogales sleeping on cardboard boxes and eating from dumps.

As I now recalled, while I had attended schools in Arizona for nearly seventeen years, I knew very little of the "history" of immigration. I didn't recall ever having covered the doctrine of "Manifest Destiny," the Mexican-American War, the "Bracero Agreement," nor "Operation Wetback" in my studies. The only thing I seemed to remember was that in 1853 the U.S. bought a parcel of land in northern Mexico which became part of Arizona, and that this sale was known as the "Gadsden Purchase." I also recalled that I learned how "my ancestors" came from England and fought a revolutionary war to be free of tyranny so that Americans could have liberty and justice for all. Later I discovered that "for all" in reality meant for a few selected Caucasian people – no freedom for black slaves, no adhering to treaties with Natives, no legal personal or property rights for "greasers" or "chinks."

In 2007 while attending classes at Adam State College, Alamosa, Colorado as a part-time student, I had ample time and resources (periodicals, books, video tapes) in the school library and was thus fortunate to be able to examine the topic of immigration in a comprehensive manner. I also attended several beneficial on-campus lectures by visiting "experts" on this subject. I even took a 2500 mile Greyhound Bus roundtrip to the border town of Calexico-Mexicali where I had grown up fifty years ago. Unfortunately, not a lot had changed, though they now did have a "**McDonald's**" on the gringo side of the river.

The writings included in this book are observations told as historical studies, poems, and factional (term borrowed from *Roots'* Alex Haley) anecdotes. As I did my studies I became aware that "average Americans," including politicians that make decisions on important immigration matters, have not put in the time nor have the resources that I did to obtain a knowledge-based view on this topic. I believe it is these same people that will then add to the confusion that will be the fuel for a giant emotional conflagration. Unfortunately our thousands of tears will barely create a wisp of damp smoke in the attempt to lift the veil of ignorance. Will we be able to extinguish the many fires to come?

Some of you will probably already know of the initial material in this study, but I feel as you continue reading, you'll be surprised as to how much of U.S. History or World History is intertwined with today's "hot" issue of immigration. It is my sincere hope that you as an educated citizen will share this material with others who could use more "luz" on the subject.

Admittedly there are undocumented workers that have come to the United States "illegally" and have committed crimes while they were here, but that is no reason to make new immigration laws that state that anyone can be stopped and detained because of "reasonable suspicion" that you are undocumented. You "look a suspicious?" What does that mean? Yes you should be deported if you are a foreign alien and have committed a serious crime. Looking for food is not in my category of a serious crime.

Proponents of these new racist laws say that this will not encourage "racial profiling." Oh? Last year I was coming back to Colorado from Arizona after attending the funeral of my dear sister. I came back by the southern route going through Las Cruces, New Mexico. After heading north on I-25, I passed an immigration check point and was "waved through." About ten miles later, I was stopped by the flashing lights of a "Migra" patrol car. I immediately asked for the reason that I had been stopped. The "officer" said that I was driving a "suspicious" vehicle and showed me a small card that said he had all the right in this world to stop me. I asked him what was so "suspicious" about my car. He said,

"First, you're driving late at night (12:30 A.M.)" And I said, "You've got to be kidding." He continued, "Secondly, you're driving too slow, 55 mph," and pointed to the 75 miles per hour sign just ahead. Now I'm beginning to get somewhat angry. I have just been to my sister's passing, I'm exhausted, and this guy is hassling me about nothing. And then he says, "Also you look 'suspicious' because you have Colorado license plates." Now, the jalapeños in my neck vein were really starting to "kick in." "YOU'VE GOT TO BE KIDDING!" He finally let me be on my way. I told him I truly didn't understand what had just happened and that this was just the sort of thing that gets me angry about in our immigration policies. I also kept my promise to him- I told him that someday I would write about him and this nonsensical incident.

As I look back at this run-in with the "Migra," there is a part that was never told. Every time, before a car is stopped, an officer does a license check on the vehicle. This check would have shown that this particular vehicle was owned by someone with the Hispanic surname of Larriva. If the "Migra" officer would have been truthful and sincere with me, he would have told me that that was the real reason I was detained. If I had been driving at 12:30 A.M., 55 miles per hour, had Colorado license plates, AND had my last name been Smith, I am certain that I would not have been stopped.

So what is going to happen with these new "suspicious" type laws, is not only can you be stopped for how you look, but also for having a "suspicious" name. As in Nazi Germany, somebody might just "turn you in" because you have a strange name or an unusual accent.

This business of "But they're breaking the law" gets pretty old for me. In the year I was conceived the white laws made it illegal for a "Yellow Nigger," or Chinaman, which my father was, to marry a Mexican "wetback." Hence through no fault of my own, this particular unjust white law made me a bastard. We need <u>Just</u> laws.

On Monday, April 26, 2010 the Arizona legislature passed an anti-immigrant legislation which, in practice, promotes racial profiling, endangers the safety of all Arizonans by creating tension between law enforcement and the community they serve, and will be economically costly to the state. SB 1070 requires local law enforcement to verify a person's immigration status on mere "reasonable suspicion." This law criminalizes: 1) being undocumented, 2) working or applying for work while undocumented, 3) helping or transporting someone who is undocumented, and 4) penalizes most documented non-citizens for not carrying immigration documents with them at all times. In addition to criminal charges, the law also imposes harsh monetary penalties on violators. However, the law is not only an attack on the undocumented. Because of the broad language allowing for warrantless arrests and verification of immigrant status by local law enforcement, all Arizonans and visitors to the state, will be subjected to additional documentation requirements and a reduced standard for searches. In a state where a majority of foreign-born immigrants are Latino, but a majority of Latinos are citizens, the likelihood of racial profiling is a dismal reality.

(Latino Forum)

The Governor of Arizona also wants teachers with "heavy"accents to be dismissed from their teaching jobs. Does that mean that the Governor of California, even though he would have a teaching degree, could not teach in Arizona; and that he would basically be considered a second class citizen because of his cool "Terminator" (Austrian) accent? I believe any laws like these should be challenged constitutionally. Freedom of speech should also protect <u>how</u> something is said. What do you do with a person with a speech disability? Do you discriminate against such people, even if they can adequately do their job? Should we dismiss gringo teachers of Spanish if they have a heavy English accent? Dios mio, ayúdanos!

"Yuma Night Crawlers"

They entered the bus in the middle of the night
All in green.
They went down the aisle asking
Are you an American citizen?
I said "Sí señor" in my best gringo accent.

The girl behind me was seventeen
Blondish, well-dressed.
She said "jyes" in her best Spanish accent.
Perhaps she should have said
"Sí señor."
The night crawlers took her away.
I still pray for her.

(No young lady for any reason should be taken out of a bus by two men in the middle of the night.)
~~~~~~~~

Ronald Reagan, "Mr. Obama, tear down this wall!"
~~~~~~~~
"The King of the Land of Thieves first rapes, kills, steals, then builds a vicious fence to protect his booty."

"Languages are Keys to the Mind"

Table of Contents

(Front/back covers, prints, sculpture) - Author

Preface – "Yuma Night Crawlers" Poem

Letter to the (Dis-?) Honorable Ken Salazar
Secretary of the Interior

Kind Sir,

I first met you in the summer of '08 when you came to our small town of Alamosa, CO. You were here to "listen" to your constituency as U.S. Senator and to gather support and votes for the then yet-elected President, Barack Obama.

I was able to speak a few private words with you about my concerns of the treatment of undocumented immigrants- how they were being treated like husbandry animals. (First we use them to toil heavily in our agricultural fields, clean our toilets, and even feed our children at their breast). Then at our whim and first xenophobic fears, after "using" and "abusing" them up for years, we decide that we want to send 12 million back to wherever they came from (and this time No G-damn Amnesty!). In this process we knowingly split up families- create terror for the U.S. born children as we deport their parents in the middle of the night. And we, who pride ourselves as the great defenders of "Human Rights" around the world. Something smells of a mighty rotten hypocrisy.

Before you left, I handed you a report I had done on Immigration which told of the many injustices the U.S. has placed upon foreigners and their countries, thus creating many immigrants that "must" go and find work elsewhere. In your general "nice man" gesture, you thanked me and "assured" me that your friend "Barack" would be "taking care of this." Kind sir, it's been two years now (almost to the day), and your friend "Barack" (admittedly he has had a "full plate") has only "taken care" of this issue by sending 1,200 soldiers to the border. Sorry to say but to many supporters this is a huge "slap in the face." It would have been better if "Barack" had done nothing. More soldiers is not the answer.

Sir, please mean what you say. Fragile lives are at stake.

Sincerely, YJF Larriva   August 2010

Part I.

"Reflections of the Racist Moon"
(It only reflects what it sees)

Bronze Moon

*"Anyone can have an opinion, but only Knowledge
will allow you to be one."*

"Guardians of the Flyway"

In the Desert, lettuce fields have no sense of
smell,
while the onion fields with their hot Dancing
mirages
outdo themselves in spectacular scents of
Heaven...
of the sweetest onions mixed with a taste
of dusty rain... Fragrant tears.

And as Hungry beaming searchlights scan
The fields narrow and wide for shifting
shadowy Trees
in darkness of morning, noon, neon night,
No one in the acequias breathes in,
a few Dare to breathe out.

From space, weightless Mirrored faces can
clearly see
the empty mouths of the shoeless,
sweating backs of those sleeping on
icy Frigidaire cardboard boxes.

The proud kerosene Lamp on the dirt floor
is indeed the Light of the World as it sneaks out
in rusty Silence past a castle of wooden crates,
tattered tin.

Once freed, the light beams shine as
Twisted patterns of gleaming Knives,
slicing into the rotting garbage Smells
of another early morning Hell.

"Remember Hijo when the Ancestors
had sworn by 'the Nopales de Nogales'
that man would always be free to wander
as the creatures in the clouds?"
Now dark Black graffiti walls,
higher than the guardian Saguaros have come
to sands of cactus storms,
spawned twisting snakes
that flow from Sea to Drowning Sea."

Worse yet, foreign nativists set traps,
capture those with thirsty desires for a better life,
find them floating as dry parchments written by
the Dead
in an Ocean without water, without hope –
Screaming in ancient, unknown tongues,
writhing naked with Mouthfuls of sand, Mad
minds,
Drinking imaginary Rainwater, For an imaginary
life.

Still more fearless birds fly North, in all Seasons
 As they attempt to recover the memories stolen
from their pasts before patched holes in
 barbed-wire Fences kept tears,
 Simple Dreams from meeting.

Fences (03/05/07)

Go right ahead. Mend your fences. Build your 800-hundred mile wall, a wall that is a mere extension of the walls in your hearts. Pacify millions of U.S. "Americans" who have truly never been hungry, nor have ever taken one step back to understand history. Do it all in the guise (disguise) of "national security." Personally, as far as being hungry, I grew up as a five-year-old child in the 1950s, on the Mexico-U.S. border towns of Nogales, Mexicali, and Tijuana. I was born in Phoenix, though my mother of Chihuahuan roots, preferred to have us wander around on Mexican soil. No father known well. Rumors are that he was from Canton, China. The mother and I slept on cardboard boxes on dirt floors, went "shopping" at the local dump, and ate what we could steal or what she could accomplish from the sale of her one-armed body. Whenever mi madre was gone on her midnight "errands," my friend the kerosene lamp and I would play shadow puppets on the cracked adobe wall. My quick fingers would make the shadow picture of a bowl of frijoles, stack of corn tortillas, verdolagas con queso, and yes, my favorite, a whole pollo asado (roasted chicken).

AWAKE IN A MEXICALI DREAM

"Are you sure he's asleep?"
whispers the gringo stranger as
he humps on my mother like
my friend Miguelito did to
the sows in the pig yard.

Of course I'm asleep.
How else could I be dreaming
about soaring to Phoenix
and beating my girl cousins
at playing jacks? I'm the champ.

If his hairy arm brushes by me
one more time, I swear I'll cut him
with the razors we tie to our kites
when we war high in the sky.

"He doesn't look asleep."
Of course I'm asleep.
How else could I be dreaming of
that hot corn on a stick sold at the
corner stand? Ay, with melted
mantequilla, dusted with salt,
chile powder…delisioso.
I've never had one before.
Perhaps now with my mother's
five new pesos, she'll buy me one.

"The noise doesn't bother him?"
Usually it did,
but this time I was ready for the creaking
of the rusty springs;
I put some tortilla masa in my ears.
I hope the cucarachas
are asleep and dreaming.

"He's waking up."
How could I be waking up
if I am dreaming that I am dead?

"More Than An American"

Recently, in the process of doing research for a book on the memoirs of a small Chino-Latino boy, many threads have lead to a history of the United States and European nations; a history, which, as a whole, has shown itself, unfortunately, I believe to be of a great racist nature. The moon sees it all. Once a month, in all its fullness, it clearly reflects back in our faces that which we try to subtlety hide or totally ignore. Before you label me as a weird, radical trouble-maker type, I want to say that I just consider myself to be a mere citizen who dearly loves his country – but just as important, I also love and have high respect for other human beings from around the world that are part of the family of man. My desire is to be **"MORE THAN AN AMERICAN."** I am neither a historian, an academician, nor a scholar. All that I am is a simple man who is walking into the 21st century with a burdened heart, a large mirror of history in his left hand, and an anxious pen in his right that keeps calling out for peace and justice for all people.

Presently, I am not an "activist type," but the more l learn of the cruelties, injustices and continuous exploitations inflicted upon the sovereign and indigenous peoples of the world by the European Caucasians and their descendants of the last 500 years, my blood is getting ready "to march." I must make it clear that I as I write this article it is not my intention to explicitly condemn a particular race, or that am I a "reverse racist," one who blindly blames white peoples for all of the world's ills. **I know that there are millions and millions of Anglos, Caucasians, gaijin, wasps, gabachos, haoles, blancos, güeros, and gringos who have white skin (like the angel of HALO Betty Tisdale), but above all, have hearts of gold and are**

**nicer and more compassionate to others than I will
ever be.** Forgive me if I am insulting anyone but… But I
become quite angry when I see undocumented workers
(human beings, just the same) from south of the border
being rounded up like cattle, not only like cattle, but
treated as sub-humans as two radio DJs in New Jersey
showed recently. They had a program called "Cuca
Gotcha," in which you could call and turn in an "illegal
immigrant." Their term "Cuca Gotcha" referred to the
Spanish word cucaracha which means cockroach.
Extremely deplorable. And they wonder why people
think that they are racist and perhaps lower than
cockroaches themselves.

Family Reunification Policy

Before I get too far of myself, since most of the writing in
this book will deal with employment of documented
and undocumented workers coming to the U.S.A., I
must first state that family reunification is the primary
criterion for immigration to the U.S. Historically, the
emphasis on family reunification in American
immigration law began in the 1965 act by allotting 74%
of all new immigrants allowed into the United States to
family reunification visas. Those included, in
descending preference, unmarried adult children of U.S.
citizens (20%), spouses and unmarried children of
permanent resident aliens (20%), married children of
U.S. citizens (10%), and brothers and sisters of U.S.
citizens over age 21 (24%).

Under the Citizen Clause of the Fourteenth Amendment
to the United States Constitution, *All persons born or
naturalized in the United States, and subject to the
jurisdiction thereof, are citizens of the United States and
of the State wherein they reside.* While the Supreme

Court has never explicitly ruled on whether children born in the United States to illegal immigrant parents are entitled to birthright citizenship via the Fourteenth Amendment, it has generally been assumed that they are, and permanent residents of the United States may sponsor relatives for immigration to the United States in a variety of ways. Citizens of any age may sponsor their heterosexual spouses and their children, **but only citizens who have reached the age of 21** may sponsor siblings and parents. Permanent residents may only sponsor spouses and unmarried children. In all cases, the sponsor must demonstrate the capacity to support their relative financially at 125% of poverty level, and provide proof of the relationship. Immediate relatives of United States citizens (spouses, parents, and unmarried children under 21 years of age) are automatically eligible to immigrate upon approval of their application. All other people eligible to immigrate through a family member must wait for a place; a preference system governs the order at which these places become available.

Having US citizen minor children has been mischaracterized as being beneficial in deportation proceedings; such benefits do not exist except in the very rare case of extreme and profound hardship on the child. The number of such hardship waivers is capped at 5000 per year. Federal appellate courts have upheld the refusal by the Immigration and Naturalization Service to stay the deportation of illegal immigrants merely on the grounds that they have U.S.-citizen, minor children.

See **Part VIII,** pg. 152 of this book **(New Issues 2010)** where Republicans are trying to deprive US newborns of undocumented immigrants of their citizenship. "We should amend the 14th Amendment so that 'Anchor Babies' or 'Drop Babies' do not automatically become US citizens," cry out these politicians as they sound out their personal political death knells. Imagine trying to make criminals out of innocent newborns! What does this have to do with securing the borders? Smoke screen for getting rid of a brown scourge?

"Operation Wetback" 1950s

Yes, today many undocumented workers are being sent back to their home countries under **"Operation Return to Sender"** (wouldn't Elvis be proud?). This is not unlike **"Operation Wetback"** of the 1950s, when the U.S. had first enticed Mexican workers to come and work in the fields due to the lack of manpower during World War II. Perhaps a more appropriate name for these workers should have been **"sweatbacks," for the baptism of wetness was not of a river, but of toil.** The following is a brief history of the "Bracero Movement" " and "Operation Wetback:"

In the early 1950s as part of Operation Wetback, la Pinche Migra had seized 280,000 illegal immigrants. By 1953, the numbers had grown to more than 856,000, and the U.S. government felt pressured to do something about the onslaught of immigration. This mind you after the U.S. government <u>enticed</u> **hundreds of thousands of Mexican field workers to come to work because of worker shortages during World War II. The majority of the workers were experienced farm laborers who came from places such as "la Comarca Lagunera" and other important agricultural regions of Mexico. Besides these experienced workers, many**

who came were common peasants who could not find work in Mexico and were forced to look for other means of survival.

They had come under "the Bracero" program, born on August 14, 1942, a so-called "embracing" solution for both countries. The braceros converted the agricultural fields of America into the most productive fields on the planet. By the 1960s, an excess of "illegal" agricultural workers along with the introduction of the mechanical harvester destroyed the practically and attractiveness of the bracero program. The program under which more than three million Mexicans entered the U.S. to labor in the agricultural fields ended in 1964. The U.S. Department of Labor officer in charge of the program, Lee G. Williams, had described it as a system of "legalized slavery," due to extremely low wages, longer than normal working hours, deplorable living conditions.

Returning to "Operation Wetback," it was a 1954 project of the "Pinche Migra" to remove illegal immigrants, primarily Mexican - known by the derogatory term "wetbacks" - from the southwestern United States. Burgeoning numbers of these immigrants prompted the "Piche Migra" along with state and local police agencies to mount an aggressive crackdown – going as far as police sweeps of Mexican-American barrios, <u>detentions, and</u> <u>ID checks of</u> <u>"Mexican-looking" people, in a region with many</u> <u>Native Americans and Native Hispanics.</u> In some cases, illegal immigrants were deported along with their American-born children, who were by law U.S. citizens.

"Operation Wetback" successfully deported approximately one million illegal immigrants in the space of almost a year. The operation was forced to end due to its perceived heavy-handed methods, which caused public outrage and accusations of police-state tactics. Where is the outrage today?

Sound familiar? This is pretty much what is still happening again today, in the year 2007, under the cold-hearted practices of I.C.E. (Immigration and Customs Enforcement.) Undoubtedly the Gestapo of Nazi Germany would have been extremely proud to see that the same techniques of terror once used upon defenseless Jewish people, were still alive and well in the United States of America, a country that boasts beamingly of its protection of human rights! The Gestapo merely justified its torturous actions by stating it was only enforcing the law and protecting the "Fatherland" from foreign enemies. Another familiar ring, resonance?

Orientals/Celestials

On another old "war" front, these same sort of injustices happened to my other ancestors, those that worked on the construction of the Transcontinental Railroad in the late 1800s. Poor Celestials in baskets were lowered down rock walls with dynamite in their teeth, in the name of Yankee ingenuity. They had the most strenuous jobs on the railroad line and got paid the least. Some are still buried in stony caved-in graves, still screaming and trying to escape. And once again, after the project was done, and the "whites" saw that the Celestials were bettering themselves and "getting ahead" – though of course these poor souls worked day and night, and for the most part for the least available wages – they created laws to exclude any more Chinese from immigrating to the "Flowery Flag Nation," as the Cantonese admiringly called America.

During the financially unstable 1870's, the Chinese became an ideal scapegoat: they were strangers, wore queues, kept to their own kind, and were very productive (conditions not inspiring great love, especially among the American laboring class). Legislation, including immigration taxes, and laundry-operation fees, were passed in order to limit the success of the Chinese workers.

Racial tensions finally snapped in 1882, and Congress passed the **Chinese Exclusion Act of 1882**, barring immigration for ten years; the Geary Act extended the act for another ten years in 1892, and by the **Extension Act of 1904**, the act was made permanent. So it was the first time a law was created to keep out a particular race. Also the members of this race were not allowed to become naturalized citizens, marry a white woman. (If a Chinaman's eyes ever saw a white woman as a wife, they were hung individually, not the eyes.) Some of my ancestors wondered:

"Why did we have to depart from the green tea of our parents and long rice of loved ones, beloved ancient homeland with smells of lotus incense, and come to stay in a place far away without celestial dragons? It is for no reason but to make a noble living. In order to survive here, we have to endure all-year-around drudgery and all kinds of hardship. We are in a continual state of seeking shelter under another person's face, at the threat of being driven away at any moment. We have to swallow down, as smelly duck pond water, the insults hurled at us."

The Journal of "Lotus Feet."

July 17, 1940 –   I came from China to the Flowery Flag Nation, but was detained at Angel Island Immigration Station, San Francisco, because of the Chinese Exclusion Act.. I came with hope in my eyes, heaviness in my heart and a pregnancy in my belly. I came "alone" looking for my beloved Kuan Yen. He had come months before and made some money to send for me. He did not tell me how he was truly admitted into the U.S. Perhaps he got in through Mexico as I have heard some Celestials come that way.   Perhaps he thought that if I showed the officials my big belly, they would have sympathy on me and let me past the Golden Gates.

July 18, 1940 –   As soon as it was announced the ship had reached America: I burst out cheering. I had found precious pearls. But now, how can I bear this detention upon arrival, doctors and immigration officials refusing to let me go? All the abuse - I can't describe it with a pen. I am held captive in a wooden barrack, like King Wen in Youli: No end to this misery and sadness in my heart.

July 20, 1940 –   I remember the moment I heard we had entered the port, I am all ready: my belongings wrapped in a bundle. Who would have expected joy to become sorrow upon sorrow Detained in a dark, crude, filthy room? What can I do? Cruel treatment, not one restful breath of air. Scarcity of food, severe restrictions – all unbearable.

Here, even our proud men bow their heads low like shameful cranes.

July 25, 1940 – In search of a pin-head gain, I was idle in an impoverished village. I've risked a perilous journey to come to the Flowery Flag Nation.

Immigration officers interrogated me; and just for a slight lapse of memory, I am deported, and imprisoned in this barren mountain. Even a brave man cannot use his might here; he can't take one step beyond the confines.

July 30, 1940 – At home I was in poverty, constantly worried about firewood and rice. I borrowed some money to come to be with Kuan Yen at Gold Mountain. Immigration officers cross-examined me; no way could I get through. Deported to this island, like a convicted criminal. Here – Mournful sighs fill the gloomy room. My nation weak; her people often humiliated like animals, tortured and destroyed at others' whims.

August 3, 1940 – Wooden barracks, all specially built; it's clear they are detention cells. We

Celestials enter this country and suffer all sorts of restrictions made at whim. What a disappointment – Cooped up inside an iron cage; We have an ambassador who cannot handle matters. We knit our brows and cry, for heaven gives no recourse for our suffering.

August 10, 1940 – The wooden cell is like a steel barrel. Firmly shut, not even a breeze can filter through. Over one hundred cruel laws, hard to list them all; Ten thousand grievances, all from the tortures day and night. Worry and more worry – How can I sleep in peace or eat at ease? There are no stocks, but the hidden punishment is just as heavy. Tears soak my clothes; frustration fills my bosom.

August 13, 1940 – Detention is called "awaiting review." No letter or message can get through to me. My mind is bogged down with a hundred frustrations and anxieties. My mouth balks at meager meals of rice gruel.
Oh, what can I do? Just when can I go ashore?
Imprisoned in a coop, unable to breathe.
My countrymen are made into a herd of cattle!

August 20, 1940 – My daughter Yu-ling came today. What a gift from the heavens! Had only her father been here. Had only she had been born in freedom in the "Land of the Free." She is so tiny. But bigger than my Lotus Feet. Thank goodness she will not have to endure the Celestials' myths on her tiny feet. Her ba-ba would be so in love with her. But I hear rumors that he might have been killed by robbers. No one is safe. Inside this cage or out. What shall we do now?

For sixty-one years, the Chinese were excluded from entering the United States and becoming natural citizens when on December 17, 1943, the United States Congress passed the **Chinese Exclusion Repeal Act**, which allowed Chinese to enter the United States legally once again. Why? Not because the U.S. had a "change of heart;" it was so the Chinese could fight and die alongside the U.S. in World War II. Yes, **"you can't Live with us, but you can Die with us."**

Japanese-American Internments

We all know that during the war with Japan, many Americans, which were of Japanese ancestry, were placed unjustly in internments camps, right? But did you know that an entire village was created for tiny Japanese American orphans by an over-crazed government with an Executive Order 9066 in hand; one then had to know the racism in the world had indeed turned itself upside down. (Read "From Manzarosa to Slab City" in Part IX Short Stories in this book.

(So you see, I am discovering that Kings like Martin Luther and princes like Malcolm X are not "born" but "made,"- their souls ignited by the blistering pyres of indignation.) Am I being too narrow in my views? See racism behind every slice of white-bread, white bed sheet with eye holes, every snow flake in "White Christmas?" Let me show you an item I just uncovered posted on the Internet. (Gregory Rodriquez (April 8, 2007): A few selections:

"Illegal? Better if you're Irish.

- An estimated 30,000 undocumented immigrants who aren't Latino live a more native-born life in New York.

Woodlawn, The Bronx - IMAGINE HILLARY Clinton holding up a T-shirt that read: "Legalize Mexicans." That's not going to happen, right? Well, last month in Washington, at a rally hosted by the Irish Lobby for Immigration Reform, the leading Democratic candidate for president actually did have her picture taken holding a shirt that read: "Legalize the Irish." That's the lobby's in-your-face slogan, which says a lot about the role that race (and ethnicity) plays in the debate about illegal immigration. Latino activists bend over backward trying to cloak undocumented Mexican migrants in the slogan "We are America," but their Irish counterparts don't feel similarly obliged.

- There are an estimated 50,000 Irish illegal immigrants in the U.S.; 30,000 of them are thought to live in New York City. Today, this tiny corner in the northern reaches of the Bronx is perhaps the most heavily Irish-born neighborhood in New York, and advocates believe that as many as 40% of local immigrants are undocumented.

- "The fact that they're white Europeans agitating for immigration reform is helpful," said Niall O'Dowd, chairman of the Irish Lobby for Immigration Reform and publisher of the Irish Voice newspaper. "Bottom line is that every ethnic group brings their own strength to the debate. We can't put a million people in the street, but we have positive political identification and a lot of access to Democrats and Republicans."

- There are 40 million Americans of Irish descent, and O'Dowd believes that a good portion of them, particularly the politicians, are sympathetic to the plight of illegal Irish immigrants. His office is filled with snapshots of him shoulder to shoulder with the likes of John McCain, Bill Clinton and Ted Kennedy. "The key is to have sympathetic politicians of the same ethnic background," he said.

- But whites' more favorable view of illegal immigrants who look like them may not translate to the growing number of Americans whose ancestors do not hail from Europe. The Pakistani-born cab driver who took me from the subway station to Katonah Avenue said he generally found Irish immigrants to be nice, as well as good tippers. "But they won't rent you an apartment around here if you're not Irish," he said. "They don't want to mix with other races."

Get the picture? Is the truth starting to focus the clouded historical lens?

Immigration in Europe
(European Union)

It should be strongly noted that the situation whereby migrating peoples who have been left impoverished by years of exploitation is not only a situation existent in the Americas. In Europe, thousands of migrants have now begun to move to the North in search of bettering their economic lives, including political ones (for many are fleeing situations which have made them refugees/immigrants) by Western exploitations. The position that Mexico plays on the U.S. border is similar to that of Turkey and Bulgaria in the East. It is there, though, where "illegal immigrants" are treated extremely harsher, due to the fact that these countries have been mandated guidelines as to future admissions to the EU. One of the foremost requirements is that they must have strictly secured borders. Some of these migrants have testified that border guards have allowed vicious dogs to bite "half a hip off." But regardless of the tortuous dangers, this emigration plight/flight continues throughout the world:

"In the waterfront street bazaars in Istanbul; the migrant ghettos of Athens; in the underworld of human smugglers; in the starving and lost young people of strife-torn Africa; those fleeing genocide; the extremely and determined poor; all continue to bravely seek stability in freedoms, wealth, and a "normalcy of life" as they desperately struggle to get to the rich countries in the West. They can daily be seen riding the dangerous rails, paddling across seas in rubber rafts, and criss-crossing snow-covered mountains on foot without maps or compasses."

For every traveler, there is an unusual story, a private view of a world most of us will never see, but yet we can be open to understand. Imagine hearing this: A story told to Behzad Yaghmaian in Turkey, 2006.

> "Did I come here illegally? Well, my feeling is that I did not cross illegally. Borders are illegal. They are not natural. Crossing them is my right. Doing what is my right is not illegal. The earth equally belongs to everyone. Borders are created by power. Have you noticed how animals make their territories by pissing on some areas? Humans are like that too: they piss and make a circle around a part of nature and make it their private territory. That is how borders are created. 'This is mine because it smells like my urine,' the government tells you."
> **(Behzad Yaghmaian-"Stories of Muslim Migrants")**

Similar to those migrant brethren in the Americas, it is if in their ardent quest for a better life, there is an underlying and subconscious "Manifest Destiny" to recover golden treasures and other riches that were "extracted" from them centuries before. These "illegal" immigrants have likewise come through extremely difficult consequences to retrieve the futures of their pasts.

Remember: The issue of Illegal Immigration is not only a National U.S. concern in the Southwest, but a World problem, initially created by the West by its unjust exploitations of Third World countries. "There are no under-developed countries, only highly exploited ones."

France: (TV) I just saw a French gendarme dragging a black African immigrant woman down a street with her baby's head bouncing up and down on the asphalt. Horrific deed. Horrific image.

Part II.

World History of Thefts in the Night
(Or world's largest gang rape.)

"Family of Man" - Cast Aluminum- 24" D.

World History of Thefts in the Night
(For they also stole the sun)

As stated before, in searching for my own past, I came across a history of a world that was full of incidents where **"Might makes Right"** and strong and rich men took advantage of the weak and defenseless. The following are brief historical examples of European imperialism and colonialism begun in the 1500s (facts which most of us know, some try to forget, others try to hide and bury in shifting sand): **World's Largest Gang Rape?**

Spanish Conquistadores (Spanish word aptly meaning conquerors) – raped and plundered most of the New World; stole the shiny, pretty gold, enslaved and killed the indigenous flesh, forced Spanish culture upon the dignity of others; left but a poisoned, denuded forest. Hooray for "Columbus Day?"

Happy COLUMBUS – Discovers' Day
OR IS IT
HAPPY CONQUEST DAY?

Happy 500+ Years of Conquest of the New Worlds

Happy 500+ years of
Deceit
Plundering
Disease
Stealing
Raping of People and Lands

Aztec Lament:
(Upside-down pyramid,
A world turned upside down?)

"Broken spears lie in the in the streets
We have torn our hair in grief
Our houses are roofless now
Our walls red with blood
Our inheritance
Our city
Is lost"
Ay

Said of Conquistador Hernán Cortés:
He obtained a hollow victory –
In achieving his dream
He had to ruin it.

Portuguese – "borrowed" African slaves, brought them and Portuguese genes in their jeans to Brazil. So thus today's ruling class in Brazil is overwhelming white.
Germans, Dutch, Belgians, Danes, Italians – continued in the spirit of the future Oklahoma "Sooners," in that they also quickly ran out to get their piece of the world pie. Africa would soon be picked of its fruit of ivory, oil, diamonds, slave manpower. (Today Africa is a dumping ground for lucrative, deadly munitions sales from the U.S., United Kingdom, France, and Germany; paid off in "blood diamonds.")
Heard of the "Belgium Congo," the "Dutch West Indies?" Check it out.

The French – Next to "Great" Britain, they were known as the largest empire. Know that they are directly related to U.S. involvement in Vietnam with their colonialism of French Indo-China? Read about it for yourselves.
And oh yes, there are our forefathers, **the British** – Supposedly they once had an "Empire on which the sun

never set." That title totally depended on which end of the whip you were on or in which shadows you hid. It could have been more aptly called by some, "the Empire on which tyranny never sets." Thank goodness for eighty-five pound weaklings like Mahatma Gandhi that had ample muscle to fight against ancient kings and queens for the independence of his beloved India. Imagine, it was illegal for the real and true Indians to gather salt in their own country, without first being heavily taxed by the British for doing so. (Today, the U.S. Empire has clutched unto the flaming torch passed on by England. Sadly, but true, "this same sun does not set on the U.S. Empire," for it has numerous military bases strategically around the world to protect "freedom" and the interests of the "American" people. Right? But, I think to some perhaps, the U.S. is more of a control freak, with its finger (trigger)] into everything – economically, politically, militarily, and even culturally.)

The British continued– dispersed themselves throughout North America, had sugar-producing colonies in the Caribbean, where slavery became central to the economy, and were at first England's most important and lucrative colonies. The American colonies provided tobacco, cotton, and rice in the south and naval material and furs in the north. Later, settlements of Australia (starting with penal colonies from 1788) and New Zealand became profitable in the exportation of wool and gold. As one can see, the British were quite adroit in planting their English seeds in foreign lands and reaping much fruit, though be it at the expense of enslaved black backs and other's fertile soil. But, one of the most egregious acts inflicted by one country on another was done by the British East India Company, between 1834 and 1860, during the two Opium Wars. At a time when the Qing Emperor declared the use of opium illegal in China, in a manner as to protect the people from a ruinous, addictive habit, the British went to war with the Chinese to compel them to buy British opium. The British won, and China lost more than a war: it lost an entire humanity, found centuries of stupor.

And why these little ventures into the past? Hopefully, it is to provide a small overview as to why we are in conflict with people we often **make strangers in their own countries**. We must come to an understanding that during the times of European world conquest, most of the riches in products of natural resources and fruits of slave manpower (perhaps billions of SMHs, stolen man hours to date) were taken back to Europe. These countries became wealthy; coffers became to bulge as well as fat stomachs wearing fat wigs. And what was given in return was usually covered in vomit, that is, the indigenous peoples were sold goods and materials that were illegal for them to get or make for themselves. What *was* distributed among the sovereign indigenous populations were feelings of second class citizenry in their own land; doctrines of racial superiority which denied the fitness of subjugated peoples for self-government; taught different positions of bowing to white skin; and programmed children of the exploited for subservient and demeaning futures of repeated history to be endured again and again. The problem is that even though we are now in the 21st century and imagine ourselves "enlightened" sorts; that is, we don't believe in slavery, that we are the "good guys" and don't exploit anyone, and of course have no racist bones in our All-American bodies, "My friends," as Pat Buchanan (we'll get to Pat later) likes to call people he doesn't yet know, we are far from being guiltless of present-day rapes, exploitations, and bigotry. A debatable statement?

The Spanish Empire

By colonizing the Americas, Spain became one of the richest and most powerful countries of the 16th century. At the height of its power in 1588, the Spanish Empire included the West Indies, Cuba, Florida, Mexico, Central America, much of South America, and the Philippines.

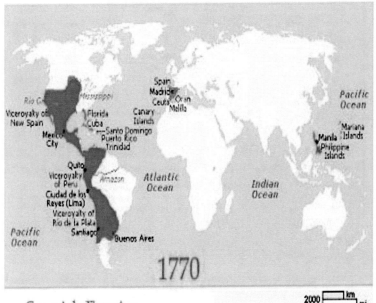

Spanish Empire

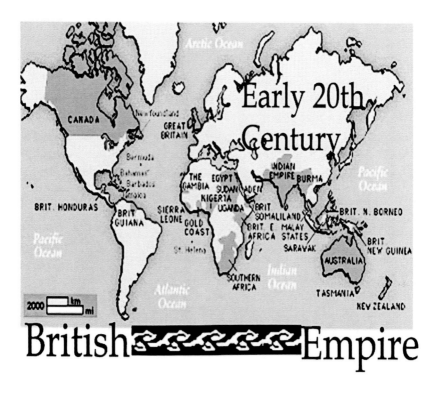

British Empire

The British Empire, established over the course of three centuries, began in the late 16th century with charted commercial ventures in sugar and tobacco plantations, slave trading, and missionary activities in North America and the Caribbean Islands. During the late 19th and early 20th centuries, the British Empire reached the height of its power, ruling over large parts of Africa, Asia, and North America.

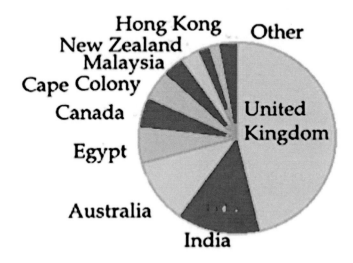

Government Revenues
of the British Empire 1905

Does the British Empire owe anything to its former colonies?

Partition of Africa 1855-1914

In 1914, every square inch of Afrika was owned by some foreign power. (See detailed color chart on back cover)

How would you like to have your country (continent) divided into foreign cemetery plots? Would any of these exploitations have dire consequences in the future of Afrika?

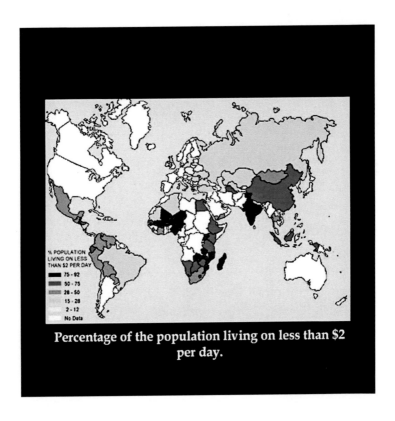

Percentage of the population living on less than $2 per day.

World Poverty - Year 2000. Is it a coincidence that the post-colonial countries are the poorest ones? The poor: We repeat, "Our countries are not under-developed, they have been merely over exploited.

Part III.

Mexico/Native Americans/Hawaii/Cuba
Mexican-American War

"Wahine with Poi Dog"-18"x24"

So friend, what do you think of this Mexican migrant who puts one foot on California, one on Arizona, one on Colorado, one on New Mexico, and two of his wet feet on Tejas, and cries out, "How can I be illegal if this land where I stand on now was stolen from my great-grandparents by the Gringo Government in 1846 in the great U.S. invasion?" You must think to yourself, "Why amigo, you must have been out in the sun too long. It is time for you to take your siesta under that jumping cholla cactus. You are muy loco!"

Truth be known, to many people, this so-called "illegal immigrant" has a strong point. Let's go back about a mere 160 years and see what truly did happen to the ancestral land of Señor Juan De Tal.

Mexican Territory in the Early 1800s, And the Texas question-

Mexican lands once extended from as far south to Guatemala in Central America, to northern areas of California, Nevada, Utah, Colorado, Arizona, Wyoming, New Mexico, and Texas. Hostilities between the U.S. and Mexico first began when Texas declared its independence from Mexico in 1836. Years prior to this time, U.S. settlers had been given permission by the Spanish Empire, which controlled all Mexico, to obtain land in Texas provided they declared themselves Catholic and manifested their obedience to the king. Before long, these New Texans, along with thousands of gringo squatters (illegal immigrants), which had come after Mexico had disallowed any more settlers, decided that they did not want to be ruled from Mexico City. Many did not like the idea that Mexico wanted them to be rid of their slaves. Slavery had continued to be a burning issue in Texas territory. Runaway slaves from the plantations of East Texas and Louisiana knew that they could find freedom across the Rio Grande. And even though patrols of vicious Texas Rangers, armed vigilantes, and the naturally wild landscape stood between them and freedom, the slaves continued to flee, often with the help of sympathetic Mexicans. The runaways were granted asylum in Mexico and a fiery gunfight was not uncommon when gringo slave hunters crossed the river in pursuit of the fugitives. Continued pressure to defend and expand the southern empire of slavery was indeed a major reason as to why the U.S. wanted to invade and conquer Mexico. The simple version of what happened next is that the New Texans fought for their "independence" from Mexico and were then annexed by the U.S. Mexico of course did not like the idea of its breakaway province becoming an American state. On **April 25, 1846**, a clash occurred between Mexican and American troops on soil claimed by both countries. **The Mexican-American War** had begun.

Manifest Destiny

The Mexican-American War was one of the major conflicts driven by the idea of "Manifest Destiny;" the belief that America had a God-given right, or destiny, to expand the country's borders from "sea to shining sea." This belief would eventually cause a great deal of suffering for many Mexicans, Native Americans, and United States citizens. By the time President Polk came to office in 1845, the idea of "Manifest Destiny" had taken root among the American people and the new occupant in the White House was a firm believer in expansion. The belief that the U.S. basically had God-given right to occupy and "civilize" the whole continent gained favor as more and more Americans settled the western lands. The fact that most of these areas already had people living upon them was usually ignored, with the attitude that democratic English-speaking America, with its high ideals and Protestant Christian ethics, would do a better job of running things than the Native Americans or Spanish-speaking Catholic Mexicans. In both 1835 and 1845, the United States, in its quest of achieving its "Manifest Destiny," offered to purchase California from Mexico, for $5 million and $25 million, respectively. Mexico refused to sell its valuable property to its dangerous and greedy neighbor. (Little did Mexico know that in the end, it would only receive $15 million for the entire package of California, Nevada, Colorado, Utah, Arizona, New Mexico, and Texas (almost half of all its territory). Not only would Mexico lose all of this land, but also two huge watering arteries; the Colorado River and the Rio Grande, that in actuality without the water from these two major streams, the acquired lands would be nearly worthless.)

"The Wolf Picks an Argument with the Lamb"

On May 13, 1846, the United States declared war on Mexico due to a skirmish on disputed land. The U.S. claimed that Mexico had "invaded our territory and shed American blood on American soil." This, not being a factual account, led to comments by some more prophetic individuals that the situation was "like the wolf picking an argument with the lamb so it could devour the whole lamb later on."

This same fear technique has been used in other more recent incidents by the US. The US bombed the crap out of Iraq looking for fabricated weapons of mass destruction. Remember?

As we recall, Mexico was vehemently opposed to selling any of its lands, but the U.S. with its "Manifest Destiny" edict in hand and powerful cannons tagging along, moved on into its **"Might makes Right"** solution. Mexico, with its recent battles of independence against European invaders, was not militarily equipped to withstand another war and consequently was defeated. Did you know that U.S. military marched all the way into the heart of Mexico? Right up to the doors of Montezuma Castle (outside of Mexico City); hence the words in the U.S. Marine Corps hymn (…from the Halls of Montezuma to the shores of Tripoli).

"All Mexico"

With American successes on the battlefield, by the summer of 1847, there were calls for the annexation of "All Mexico," particularly among Eastern Democrats, who argued that bringing Mexico into the Union was the best way to ensure future peace in the region. Many of the American field commanders who participated in the invasion of Mexico supported total annexation.

But guess what. Not all of Mexico was raped. Why? Because…This was a controversial proposition for two reasons: First, idealistic advocates of Manifest Destiny like John L. O'Sullivan had always maintained that the laws of the United States should not be imposed on people against their will. The annexation of "All Mexico" would be a violation of this principle. And secondly, the annexation of Mexico was controversial because it would mean extending U.S. citizenship to millions of Mexicans.

Senator John C. Calhoun of South Carolina, who had approved of the annexation of Texas, was opposed to the annexation of Mexico, as well as the "mission" aspect of Manifest Destiny, for **racial reasons**. He made these views clear in a speech to Congress on January 4, 1848:

> **We have never dreamt of incorporating into our Union any but the Caucasian race — the free white race. To incorporate Mexico, would be the very first instance of the kind, of incorporating an Indian race; for more than half of the Mexicans are Indians, and the other is composed chiefly of mixed tribes. I protest against such a union as that! Ours, sir, is the Government of a white race.... We are anxious to force free government on all; and I see that it has been urged ... that it is the mission of this country to spread civil and religious liberty over all the world, and especially over this continent. It is a great mistake.** (Sounds a bit like the Middle East, Mr. Pat Buchanan?)

This debate brought to the forefront one of the contradictions of Manifest Destiny: on the one hand, while racist ideas inherent in Manifest Destiny suggested that Mexicans, as non-Anglo-Saxons, were a lesser race and thus not qualified to become Americans, the "mission" component of Manifest Destiny suggested that Mexicans would be improved (or "regenerated," as it was then described) by bringing them into American democracy. Racism was used to promote Manifest Destiny, but, as in the case of Calhoun and the resistance to the "All Mexico" movement, racism was also used to oppose Manifest Destiny. (Thank God for racism?)

Treaty of Guadalupe Hidalgo (El Gran Rip-Off)

The Treaty of Guadalupe Hidalgo ended the Mexican-American War, and resulted in the U.S. taking undisputed control of Texas, taking all of California, Nevada, Utah, and parts of Arizona, New Mexico, and Wyoming. It also established the U.S.-Mexican border at the Rio Grande River. This exchange was known as the Mexican Cession (El Gran Rip-off). Lost to Mexico were the fertile coastal plains of Texas and California and the bountiful high plains of the Edwards and Colorado plateaus and the *Llano Estacado,* vast areas that have produced enormous wealth in minerals, oil, beef, cotton, corn, sugar, and other agricultural commodities. Gone were the fecund Central Valley in California, Gila River Valley in Arizona, the Mesilla Valley in New Mexico, and Rio Grande Valley in Texas; cornucopias that would come to feed so much of the U.S. population. Stolen from the Mexican people were the treasures of the Sierra Nevada, the lower Rocky Mountains, and the upper portions of Sonora and Chihuahua that have produced copious amounts of gold, silver, copper, and other minerals. In return for having its lands lifted, Mexico received a mere $15 million dollars. (Isn't this like someone admiring your nice new car that cost you $15,000, and then asks you sell it to him? Then when you refuse, he comes with his father General Cannon, gives you $5,000, and just takes it. Again, **"Might makes Right**?") If the figure $15 million seems low, it definitely was, for we had once offered $300 million for just one island, Cuba. The new treaty was signed by Nicholas Trist on behalf of the United States on February 2, 1848, at the main altar of the old Cathedral of Guadalupe at

Villa Hidalgo, north of Mexico City. It was subsequently ratified by the United States Senate on March 10, 1848 and by the Mexican government on May 19, 1848; the countries' ratifications were duly exchanged on May 30, 1848. **However, the version of the treaty ratified by the United States Senate eliminated Article 10, which stated that the U.S. government would honor and guarantee all land grants awarded in lands ceded to the United States to citizens of Spain and Mexico by those respective governments.** (My simple mind wonders if this treaty is truly valid or could it be still declared null and void by an international court of justice.) Article 8 guaranteed that Mexicans who remained more than one year in the ceded lands would automatically become full-fledged American citizens or they could declare their intention of remaining Mexican citizens; however, this Article was effectively weakened by Article 9, written into the treaty by the U.S. Senate, which stated that Mexican citizens would "be admitted at the proper time," to be judged of by the Congress of the United States. This "promise" never happened. Still waiting.

Although the Treaty of Guadalupe-Hidalgo promised that Mexicans who stayed in the Southwest would receive "all the rights of citizens of the United States," that promise was not completely fulfilled. At best, those Mexican-Americans became second-hand citizens. At worst, many became victims of overt racial and ethnic prejudices. After the treaty, many of the 75,000 Mexicans that chose to remain on land that had become part of the United States lost their own properties to unscrupulous politicians and lawyers who used their inherent knowledge of the English (English Only) language as a <u>secret weapon</u> to separate them from their ancestral holdings. To date, many descendants of those that had original deeds and land

grants from that period are still actively trying to reclaim what was stolen by Caucasia America.

Afterthoughts – Ulysses S. Grant, writing 18 years after the Mexican-American War. **"I regard the War as one of the most unjust ever waged by a stronger against a weaker nation."** Others agreed with him and felt that the U.S. had been at fault. "The U.S. has failed to live up to its ideology of democracy and freedom."

Antonia Castañeda (Historian) – "The Mexican-American War not only created military violence, but a greater **violence of the soul/spirit**. And we must live with the consequence of that violence until today. We must come to terms with it." To me, what Antonia Castañeda has said is extremely insightful. For as you can see, I've personally viewed what the U.S. (my country) has done to many lands as a violent crime of rape. And as anyone or anything that has experienced such a vicious act knows and says that they feel terribly violated, forced to do something without their will and then left in great distress. The victim is left in such trauma that it sometimes takes years, centuries to achieve any semblance of normalcy, recovery.

Texas Rangers (Los Diablos Tejanos or Los Pinche "Rinches") –
Unfortunately, the U.S. conquest of Mexico is not complete without mentioning some atrocious accounts of the rogue Texas Rangers, dubbed Los Diablos Tejanos by the Mexicans they terrorized. These pinche "rinches" were paramilitary gangs that conducted a campaign of death and destruction in the Mexican countryside, which left a legacy of hate, which is said to survive to this day. Los Diablos killed and pillaged indiscriminately. On July 9, 1846, George Gordon

Meade, a young officer who, like Grant and Lee, served as a general later in the Civil War, described this incident concerning misconduct of the Rangers:

> They have killed five of six innocent people in
> the street, for no other
> object than their own amusement…. They rob
> and steal the cattle and
> corn of the poor farmers, and in fact act more like
> a body of hostile Indians
> than civilized Whites.

Another similar story of the times:

> Texas Rangers… were mostly made up of
> adventurers and vagabonds… The gang of
> miscreants under the leadership of this Mustang
> Gray, were of this description. This party, in
> cold-blood, murdered almost the entire male
> population of the rancho of Guadalupe, where
> not a single weapon, offensive or defensive,
> could be found! Their only object was plunder!

Native Americans

For all the positive, though delusional, atmosphere and grand spirit "Manifest Destiny" created, it also created a deeply dark shadow in American History, the near annihilation of the Native American. While the positive side of "Manifest Destiny" was a surge of enthusiasm and energy for pushing west, the negative side was the belief that the white man had the right to destroy anything and anyone – namely Natives – who got in the way. Tracing the path of "Manifest Destiny" across the West would highlight mass destruction of tribal organizations, confinement of Natives to reservations, and in some cases complete genocide of some tribes. (Heard said of Colonel Chivinton in Colorado upon attacking defenseless Native women and children, "Kill them all. Nits breed lice!")

18" x 24"

Chief Joseph

The Last Drum Beat

The last drum beat is
As the last teardrop in time,
Falling into a diseased sewer
Making ripples that lead to nowhere,
Return as injured echoes, broken promises,
Ghostly memories from a not so distant past.

Sacred Tears from two warm winds,
Icy clouds, once gathered from every tribe,
Filled every stream, every river,
Melted into a roaring waterfall, Braided themselves
Into a pool pretending to be Heaven –
Though truly a whirlpool of a living Stench.

"See this buffalo nickel, my son?
Take it. Remember it.
Press it hot on your chest.
Burn it many, many times,
Thousands of times,
Then you'll see the sea
Of the rocking buffalo running the dance
That once gave us life."

The Peoples of Flesh have now been cleansed,
Purified, not by fire
But by searing lies
That bathed themselves in
The wolf skins of assimilation as
Devil schools stole our children,
Called our seeds by unknown, forgetful names.

The native body was not always perfect,
But at least it knew its purpose –
The full beat of/for life.
Hands that once flexed the bow
Now tip liquid poison that blurs,
Stumbles, erases the target.
Feet that were used to float, Burn the wind
On waves of grass,
Now but steam on cemented trails,
Called to die behind an evil plow.

Ears that listened For the heavenly hawk,
Now sadly hear echoes of city sirens,
Wailing the news of another cursed suicide.
Mouths with lips of white that chanted
Hundreds of unwritten tales
Now but silenced phantom voices-
As the blue tongues
 Of others slowly killed our language,
As well as our past,
For without language, There is no one to remember."

Eyes that traveled for miles
Captured beauty in the land, the beast,
The distant rain clouds,
Now have learned to stoop, stare silently
Into long shadows –
Suffer alone in the dark.

Hearts that once roamed free
Mated with the sacred forest,
Now have reservations behind iron bars,

Live in dog cages made of foreign laws.

Should we be free of hate?
When the victors parade themselves
Wearing cut-out virgin wombs,
When children's eyeless heads
Are but trophies on a Calvary belt?
When the majestic antlers of the elk are stolen,
Its life is left to bleed, rot
And starve the hearts, future of our youth?

Was the first drum beat destined to be the last?
The smell of wet sand in the foreign glass knew –
For though the ancient drum beat its faithful
beat,
Created living nations upon the ages,
A new cadence prophesied the coming
Of an angry fist –
Bursting through the drum skin,
Into blood-filled injustices
Of a gray future, Deep into an end.

Yes the last drum beat sounded
Out its fury, in thunder, in lightening,
Ran as a violent wind gasping – without breath,
Dragged itself into the last Trail of Tears,

Beat until its heart stopped beating –
As silence, without whispers,
Sealed a past forever, Broke the drum.

*"The white man once came to trade, now he
comes to fight and kill. He covers his face with
clouds of jealousy and tells us to be gone."*
- Sitting Bear -

~ Hawaii ~ Stolen Aloha

Did the wagon wheels of "Manifest Destiny" creak and stop at the Pacific shores? Not really, for you see it wasn't a mere addiction of all that was in between "from sea to shining sea." As most junkies know, once you taste of a new euphoria, it is almost impossible to go back to the status quo; you must have more, more, more. Thus the U.S. sought to satisfy its newly acquired sweet tooth by stretching its long probing white finger, and biting wide into the Sandwich Islands.

The "annexation" of the Hawaiian Islands on July 7, 1898, was the culmination of more than fifty years of growing U.S. commercial interests in Hawaii. During the second half of the nineteenth century, white American investors in the sugar industry gradually increased their control over the island's economic and political life. In 1887 they arranged to overthrow the local rulers and establish a government more favorable to their interests. But in 1891 they suffered a setback, when the new queen, Liliuokalani, replaced the liberal constitution they had secured with one giving her extensive power; one that gave the Native peoples more control of their own lives.

Hawaiian dissenters –
Hawaiian loyalists were extremely vocal about their sovereignty issues and were not afraid to go "brain to brain" with the "haoles" from the mainland. **James Kaulia** was a prime example. Kaulia, President of the Patriotic League (Hui Aloha Aina) declared, "The destiny of Hawaii, is situated in the mid-Pacific as she is, should be that of an independent nation, and so she would be were it not for the policy of greed which pervades the American legislators and the spirit of

cowardice which is in the breasts of those who first consummated the theft of Hawaiian prestige." "And why this greed for the Hawaiian Islands?" Kualia continued. "Is it a naval station that is needed? For that it would seem that American home ports are much in need of such protection. Is it a coaling station that is desired? That is obtainable by treaty. Or is it the islands' wealth that America desires? **If so, then America will desire to annex the earth.**" Kaulia closed in saying, "Ask for the voice of Hawaii on this subject, and **you will hear it with now uncertain tones ring out from Niihau to Hawaii, 'Independence now and forever.'**"

Unfortunately, the conch shell sound of victory was drowned out again by the booming cannons of **"Might makes Right."**

Soon a revolutionary "committee of safety," organized by Sanford B. Dole and apparently supported by the U.S. minister to Hawaii, called in U.S. Marines from a nearby cruiser (**ostensibly to protect American lives**) and established a new government with Dole as president. The U.S. minister, on his own authority, recognized the new provisional government and proclaimed Hawaii an American protectorate on February 1, 1893, completely obliterating Hawaiian sovereignty and "dumping it into the Ala Wai canal."

Dole's representatives submitted a draft treaty of annexation to the U.S. Senate, but Democratic opponents managed to delay approval until Grover Cleveland became president in March. Cleveland immediately ordered an investigation, which revealed that the **revolution had been imposed by the sugar planters and that most Hawaiians did not want annexation.** A new U.S. minister was sent to Hawaii, instructed to restore Queen Liliuokalani to the throne on condition that she reinstate the liberal 1887 constitution. President Dole, however, refused to step aside; he continued to rule and in 1894 proclaimed the independent Republic of Hawaii. Unwilling to dislodge the government by force, Cleveland reluctantly recognized it, but he refused to approve annexation.

His successor, President William McKinley, however, negotiated a new treaty in 1897. Although Democrats and anti-imperialists delayed its ratification for more than a year, the use of the U.S. naval base at Pearl Harbor during the Spanish-American War dramatized Hawaii's strategic importance. When it became clear that the administration still could not get the two-thirds vote necessary for ratification, annexation was approved instead by joint resolution of Congress, which required only a majority vote. In 1900, Hawaii was made a territory, with Dole as governor. In 1959, it was admitted as the fiftieth state in the Union. (I had always wondered why I always gagged and felt thorny spines down my throat whenever I ate a Dole pineapple. Now I know the reason why; it was history telling me to "Wake up and extend a helping hand to the Native Hawaiians in their fight for justice and their call for their own sense of "Manifest Destiny," – for some form of "Regal Restitution." By the way, the correct pronunciation for the word "Hawaii," is "Havaii." Written w's are pronounced as v's. **Imperialism not only steals, but also denies the existence of others.**

The "Great" U.S. Empire

All of the whole world thinks of the United States today as an empire, except the people of the United States,"' wrote *New York Times* columnist Walter Winchell in **1927**. "We shrink from the word 'empire,' and insist it should not be used to describe the dominion we exercise from Alaska to the Philippines, from Cuba to Panama, and beyond." "Nevertheless," he added, "we control the foreign relations of all the Caribbean countries; not one of them could enter serious relations abroad without our consent. We control the relations with each other. We exercise the power of life and death over their governments in that no government can survive if we refuse it recognition. We help in many of these countries to decide what they call their elections, and we do not hesitate, as we have done recently in Mexico, to tell them what constitution we think they ought to have. Whatever we may choose to call it, this is what the world at large calls an empire, or at least an empire in the making. Admitting that the word has an unpleasant connotation, nevertheless it does seem as if the time has come for us to look the whole thing squarely in the face and to stop trying to deceive ourselves."

Ay! In 1927! Yes to some, it was so darn obvious that Uncle Sammy was eating all the spinach in the world and changing himself not to cool Popeye, but into the "Incredible Hulk." Here I must mention Cuba. Not only because of the early injustices it suffered in 1895, but also more importantly for the cruelty its citizenry (especially children) have had to endure at the capriciousness of the U. S. for the last half a century at the expense of the **Cuban blockade** – a mere 90 miles off the coast of Florida.

Cuba, Cuba, Cuba (The Little Hostage Sister)

The United States and Cuba have a long history of close economic and political ties. Though Cuba had been a Spanish colony for nearly 400 years, the island had developed increasing trade links with the United States during the 19th century. In 1898, Spain "ceded" control of Cuba to the U.S. following its defeat in the Spanish-American War. The U.S. consequently granted Cuba its independence in 1902, yet frequently intervened in Cuban political affairs.

The Cuban Revolution of 1959 saw the overthrow of General Fulgencio Batista and rise to the power of Fidel Castro. The U.S. government formally recognized the new Cuban administration, but relations were soon to deteriorate as the Cuban government passed the first Agrarian Reform Law, allowing for the re-expropriation of large-scale (largely American-owned) land holdings. How dare the Cubans to desire land that was basically stolen by rich land owners allied to American interests! During 1960, tensions between Cuba and the U.S. escalated into economic warfare. Each time the Cuban government nationalized American properties (though Cuba did offer some payment for U.S. holdings), the American government in response to that, took countermeasures, resulting in the prohibition of all exports to Cuba on October 19, 1960.

The fact that the U.S. did not impose sanctions to many other dictatorships, some of which the U.S. supported, lead some scholars to believe that the reason for the embargo was revealed in a declassified 1964 State Department document which declared Fidel Castro to be an intolerable threat because he **"represents a successful defiance of the United States, a negation of our whole hemispheric policy almost a century and a half,"** since the Monroe Doctrine. (The doctrine was piece of American paper basically stating that no other nation in the World could deal with any country in the Americas, North or South, except the U.S.!)

This current embargo clearly shows that it is an embargo specifically directed not at a country, though its people have been greatly punished by it, but at a man – a mere caricature of a small man puffing on one of his treasured cigars, as smoke forms a big **NO MÁS (NO MORE).** How dare he say NO to the Great America! Sounds like another cartoon character, one in Venezuela?

I have included this small history of U.S.-Cuban relations in this book to show and point out some of the inconsistencies and perhaps hypocritical notions of our "American Democracy." The simple point is this: **The United Nations General Assembly has passed a non-binding resolution condemning the embargo every year since 1991. The most recent condemnation took place on November 8, 2006, by a vote of 183-4, with the U.S., Israel, Palau, and the Marshall Islands voting against.** By a vote of 183 to 4! Since the last 16 years! And the embargo bill could not be repealed! What does democracy mean then? Besides literally meaning, "Government by the People," in spirit, it doesn't it also mean, "Rule by Majority?" Again, **"Might makes Right,"** rears up its ugly two-faced head. Wouldn't it be grand if Cuban families could count on a "pollo in every pot," at least once in every two years? More questions, "What color are Cubans?" How about Eskimos? We won't go there for now, but perhaps you should.

Part IV.

Religion and Immigration
"The American Dream"

"'Every Knee' after A. Durer" - 24"x 36"

(Why tie these two together? Because millions of religious stones are being cast unjustly at the poor from many Sunday school baskets.)

Attention: "Born-Againers" or Religious Stones

What say ye on the issue of undocumented immigrants? I can pretty much assume that most of you, being good-law-abiding citizens, will loudly yell it from the rooftops like good Pharisees, "They must obey the law! Unclean, unclean, unclean! They must obey the law!" Wait un momento. Let's look at some of our Bible characters. Moses, the man chosen by God to deliver His people, murdered an Egyptian. Should we send Moses back to historical Egypt and have him stand trial? He did break the law. Perhaps he had a loophole though; the Law (Ten Commandments) had not been given yet. How about King David? He saw a beautiful babe bathing on a rooftop, and most absolutely had to "have" her. After he discovered that the married woman had become "with child," his child, he called for her soldier husband from the front lines to come and be with her. But guess what? The guy did not go home, but slept on the doorstep of his house for he felt he could not have such privileges while his men were fighting in battle. So then to creatively solve his problem, the king ordered him to go to the most extreme front trenches, where he would have a guarantee of certain death. And it was so. Should we try, convict King David, "the man after God's own heart," for first committing adultery and then murder? I believe that in both cases, Moses and King David received great doses or outpourings of <u>amazing grace</u>. **Is it grace that is most needed today in the case of many individuals that who haven't murdered anyone, and are merely trying to feed their families?**

By the way, the soldier sacrificed in the story was named Uriah, <u>my</u> favorite Bible character.

The rooftop Pharisees continue shouting, "But they are illegal, unclean, illegal," as they point their crooked fingers at a humanity scurrying to find food. "Legality" again is a matter of who is holding the law book in one hand and the biggest gun in the other. What is truly "illegal" at this point in history is not a neighboring people, but a "War" that was begun against Iraq by the United States. Yes, Mr. Hussein was a terrible person, perhaps a butcherous criminal. But the U.S. had no "legal right" to bomb his suspected locations, killing hundreds of innocent people in the misdirected process of killing him. (Tell me honestly, people injured in "collateral damage" don't bleed, don't die, don't curse us from their graves?) Who were the true terrorists in this case? Nobody stopped us. Our country is too powerful for others to say nay to us. And when they do not agree with us, we just ignore them (like also in the Cuban blockade) and continue on our unjust ways. Sorry to disagree with a lot of you, but killing innocent people is not legal, nor is it "Godly." Yes, many of us can point a finger at the law-breakings of these migrants, but perhaps we should point many more at ourselves when we steal Native lands, we cheat on our taxes, cheat on our spouses, skip out on paying our bills, buy illegal drugs (**though we attack the "illegal aliens" who supply them**), solicit a prostitute, drive drunk, break the speed limit, and even injure our brothers and sisters with our murderous thoughts. We let our baseball, Tour de France heroes, use illegal substances. Wall Street tycoons receive legal, but "obscene" bonuses. (But it's not the same? Really? Breaking some is OK?) Remember Jesus and the woman caught in adultery?

The Law said to stone her. Where was the guilty man? **Law vs. Justice** – I'll choose **Justice** every time.

Let's look at this religion and undocumented immigrant topic further. Do the sacred writings cover any of this? How about Exodus 22:21? It states, **"Do not mistreat an alien or oppress him for you were once aliens in Egypt."** Is this pertinent here? I believe that it is, since in principle, we, or our ancestors, were once aliens and have found shelter here in America. I understand that not everyone who wants to be in the U.S. can be here. But, what about the ones that are already here? Sorry to point out that much of these illegal immigration problems have been our fault. For years we have indeed invited peoples from the South (Mexico, Honduras, Guatemala, et al) to come and do the most menial and filthy jobs (and historically pay them the least). Now that some U.S. citizens are feeling threatened from "without and within," have been presented "convenient" and racist excuses through security of the homeland, we have decided to deport them all without consideration for the many inhumane situations that we are creating (in fact terrorizing) for many families. How do you think it must feel to a child to have a loved one stripped from them in the middle of the night, perhaps never to see them again? (Personally, my heart has known this.) Isn't this oppressing the alien? We must cease and desist from doing these atrocious acts immediately before there are severe repercussions. Unfortunately it seems that daily, we are making thousands of enemies all over the world. Whenever we have the opportunity to place goodness upon evil and ignore it, sadly, such fruit sowed will only be sorrow upon sorrow. When in doubt, don' know what to do – just love. "Love covers a multitude of sins." No?

Most of you know the scripture in Luke 10:27, **"Love the Lord, your God with all your mind, heart, soul, strength; and love your neighbor as yourself."** So, who is our neighbor? It could be those neighbors south of the border and or anyone who is in need of our help. And how should we love them? I think it means "as selfishly as we care about ourselves." Hard stuff. But he, who has an ear, let him hear. (Recently in my observations as to how some "religions" are handling the matter of "illegal immigration," I have come to notice that the Catholic folk have done much in handing out their hearts to their "neighbors." Besides having created "half-way homes" and held forums for migrants (documented or undocumented), they have clothed and fed many that have needed sanctuary in Bethel, the "house of God." Keep up the kind work.

The following is a story heard around a border campfire:

A migrant from the South and his pregnant wife on a donkey were traveling through a small U.S. country neighborhood. The family had traveled for literally thousands of miles, when they had no food or water for them or their beast. On the road that they traveled lived a minister on one side and a peasant farmer on the other. Having no water for him and his wife, the migrant asked the "man of God," for some refreshment for his wife. The "religious" man thought, "If I help them, more of them will just keep coming, and I also will be breaking the law and be incarcerated." So he refused to help, and just said, "Lo siento." So the migrant man also asked the peasant farmer for some agua, thinking, though, that he too would refuse him. But the farmer said, remembering when he was once in great need, "You people come here, trample on my flowers, scare my animals, leave gates unlocked and my only horse is lost, but I understand your world. Here, eat this loaf of bread, take my cup of grape Kool-Aid. It will heal your broken body. Go in peace. Remember me Always." (A kind of communion?) **So, my friends, who did the will of God, the religious leader or the peasant?**

"American Dream"

I have heard this particular scripture tossed about, (even by some politicians), **"From him who has been *given* much, much is expected."** The U.S. has been "given" much. We live the **"American Dream."** This dream calls for three cars in a two-car garage; his and hers bathrooms <u>inside</u> the house, an electricity-guzzling plasma TV in every other room; a refrigerator full of food from such exotic places like Guatemala, Argentina, Mexico; and a crab-grass-less two-story home in a cozy cul-de-sac. We go on vacation with a 30-foot RV, pulling a Jeep, that's pulling a motorboat, that's pulling two mountain bikes. Are we expected to give any of our marbles back? I believe the answer is, "Yes," (at least a few) for *"From him who has not been given, but has stolen, exploited, cheated, much will certainly be demanded?"* (Unholy version?) I believe that in most courts of law, when someone steals a commodity from another individual, the perpetrator is either incarcerated, made to present restitution, or both. Much has been stolen by the Caucasian Nations, too often from the poorest of the poor. (In this case, I too consider myself guilty.) I understand that it is difficult to return the specific stolen items to their rightful owners, but I know that with a kind, creative heart we can make some form of restitution for many of our crimes. But it all begins with the knowledge, based on the truth of history, **that yes we all ripped off a lot of people in our climb to the top.** (We, the U.S. with only a fifteenth or less of the world population, use up fifty percent of the world's resources, resources which we quickly turn to useless mountains of trash and garbage. Nothing particularly evil about this, only that we have somehow stepped on many foreign hearts to get to our lofty perch.)

WWtMD—
(What Would the Messiah Do?)

*"I was thirsty and you did not give me drink.
I was hungry and you did not give me bread.*

I was naked and you did not clothe me."

"Lord, when were you thirsty, hungry, and naked?"

"When you put me behind your fences."

"El Sueño"

"I Have Had a Dream"

In August of 1977 I had a dream, or was I merely dreaming that I was in a dream? In the dream it was 1985, and I was looking over the shoulder of an artist "friend," Howard, and he was writing up a storm. He was writing as quickly as he could his account of having had an encounter with the "Prophet of Prophets." He was now on page 47. His pen quickly and firmly wrote down what the "The Prophet of Prophets" had told him:

"The United States has been given the opportunity to be the teacher for the world, but much is expected of those to whom much has been given. The United States has been given more of everything than any country in the history of the world and it has failed to be generous with the gifts. If the United States continues to exploit the rest of the world by greedily consuming the world's resources, the United States will have God's blessing withdrawn. Your country will collapse economically which will result in civil chaos. Because of the greedy nature of the people, you will have people killing people for a cup of gasoline. The world will watch in horror as your country is obliterated by strife. The rest of the world will not intervene because they have been victims of your exploitation. They will welcome the annihilation of such selfish people. The

United States must change immediately and become the teachers of goodness and generosity to the rest of the world. Today the United States is the primary merchant of war and the culture of violence that you export to the world. This will come to an end because you have the seeds of your own destruction within you. Either you will destroy yourselves or God will bring it to an end if there isn't a change."

He continued writing feverishly:

"The United States has been given the opportunity to be the peacemaker of the world. With its medical, agricultural, manufacturing, and scientific knowledge, America could teach less fortunate countries how to give every person food, clothing, housing, medical care, education, and economic prosperity. The United States has the power to help every person in the world access clean water and hygiene waste disposal. Millions of people in the world are dying for lack of things that the people in the United States take for granted. This is not God's will. God wants you to know that every person in the world is your brother and sister. God wants every person to have the same chance for fulfillment that a person in America has. God sees the people of the

United States becoming greedy, self-centered, and uncaring. There must be a turning to God, or the reign of the United States will end. By the way, the question you asked me about which is the best religion? The greatest religion is the one that gets you closer to God."

(**Howard Storm-** *"Second Chance"* **1985**)

To say the least, this was an interesting and powerful dream. This dream changed my life. It helped me to see what is truly important in my relationship with my God and others. Can dreams be life-changers? Just ask the followers of Dr. M. L. King Jr.

Part V.

English-Only, Spanish, Bilingualism, "Ugly American"

"Gemini Language Glyph"
Burnished Earthenware- 28" H.

"English-Only"- (lingua franca)
or "The French Language" is now English

(Or now that Salsa is the number one condiment in the U.S., let's declare a law that makes Salsa the "National Condiment.")

Before I begin examination of this other difficult and controversial subject, I must tell you that my first language was Spanish. It was not by choice, as most things are in the beginnings of our lives. I am not necessarily "proud" that I speak Spanish, nor am I "proud" that I speak English. What I would have been extremely proud of is that if I had taken it upon myself to have learned another language such as French or Chinese, some language that I would have had to "work at/for," not merely acquired by me "naturally." I believe that the more languages one knows, **the more views he can have into the soul of man.**

As I mentioned before, I was born in Phoenix but roamed around with mi madre around the dump piles of the U.S.-Mexico border towns. It was decided that I, without mi madre, should live in the projects in Phoenix with my older sister and her husband so that I could go to school in the U.S. I was eight years old and placed in the first grade because I did not know any English. The teacher "recognized" right away that I was "deaf," for that's how I must have appeared to her. (My face was merely trying to catch all of the new sounds in the room. I was in a world of loud silent noise.) She could also tell that I did not know how much fun "Dick and Jane" were having teaching other "gringuitos" how to read. So... she put me in a dark closet. I was not afraid for it smelled like the ancient rivers of my Méjico. I did not cry for I could see my future in a little bit of light that sneaked underneath the door. I also smiled for I remembered the story of our neighbor's pigeon:

"El Pichón"

Vuela, vuela pichón cabrón
Paras todos los días en el buzón.
Tienes alas que te llevan aquí y ahí,
Eres del vecino y no de mí.

Mi madre tiene hambre y así es la cosa,
No me deja jugar con mis mariposas.
Quiere que to mate pichón cabrón
Y te comemos solos en el rincón.

Tus plumas tiré anoche a Los Estados
Unidos
Pero el viento las trajo con poco de ruido.
Plumas, plumas aquí y ahí.
¿Crees que saben que te comí?

"The Pigeon"

Fly, fly damn pigeon
You land everyday on the mailbox
You have wings that take you here, there
 Everywhere
 You belong to the neighbor and not to
me
My mother is hungry and this is the thing
She doesn't let me play with my butterfly
wings
She wants me to kill you damn pigeon
And we'll eat you in the corner all alone.

Last night I threw Your feathers to the
United States side,
But the wind brought them back
Quietly, with little noise.
Feathers here and there, everywhere.
Do you think they know that I ate you?

True pigeon story. "Sounds" much better in Spanish.

U.S. Peace Crops

After graduating from college I joined up with the U.S. Peace Corps and went to the Philippines. Did you know that the Philippines are named after a king in Spain after Spain helped itself to its 7,000 plus islands? Did you know that English is the "lingua franca" there? Kind of amusing, English is now becoming the "French language" around the world. You can pretty much go from one end of the Philippines to the other and be able to use English and be understood. It is used in all the banks, other institutions without any paranoia or xenophobic entanglements. Oh that reminds me, they will also accept U.S. dollars, as most countries do around the world. I mention this because recently in the U.S., a pizza chain called "Pizza Patrón, ("Boss Pizza," cool name) began to accept Mexican pesos as payment and afterwards started receiving "death threats." Oh my goodness, how insular! Is this a correct way to express this? My English, she is not so good. It is also a fact that the Canadian dollar is accepted in many of the Northeast businesses near the Canadian-U.S. border. I guess that there is no problem here for both of these countries have "white" dollars.

"The Ugly American"

It was in the Philippines that I first became acquainted with the **"Ugly American,"** that loud, annoying, boisterous know-it-all, which the locals "tolerate," but can't stand. When the horrible and tragic incident occurred in 9/11, I quietly understood why. Unfortunately, most Americans do not realize how terribly we can incense some foreigners, especially in their own country. We butcher their language, spit out their food, trample upon their customs, and laugh at their religions, not their jokes – all in front of their very eyes. Though of course, this not enough reason for anyone to retaliate in murderous, terrorist acts. I recommend that anyone wanting a good perspective as to how we can achieve a higher degree of diplomacy around our fragile world, commodity desperately needed today, read the *"Ugly American"* by Eugene Burdick and William J. Lederer, 1958. Even though the book is in the form of a novel and was written almost fifty years ago, I feel it contains an invaluable and universal wisdom that can prevent some of the blunders we are continuing to make year after year in dealing with foreign countries. Unfortunately we have left such wisdom in our historical bookshelves and have allowed our politicians' ignorance of foreign affairs lead us into 20-30 year-old patterns of disaster. The top priority in diplomacy? First learn each other's language. It is also imperative to quickly realize that many foreign businessmen and leaders perceive Westerners as:

- Acting superior; knowing the answers to everything
- Not wanting to share credit for accomplishments of joint efforts

- Being unable to respect and adjust to local customs and culture
- Preferring solutions based on their home cultures rather than meeting local needs
- Resisting working through administrative, legal, channels, and procedures
- Managing in an autocratic and intimidating way
- Being too imposing and pushy

(An excellent resource for cross-cultural training is the book *Intercultural Services: A Worldwide Buyer's Guide Sourcebook* by Gary Wederspahn.)

After Peace Corps, I chose to return and live in Hawaii, where I had trained for PC before going to the Philippines. I must confess that I returned to Hawaii instead of Arizona because I felt more comfortable there, since I have oriental-type features. I had gotten tired of always having to "prove myself," to and in Caucasian America before being accepted as a normal person. After a while one gets sick of this sort of discrimination. Oh, it was so nice to have the lady at the cafeteria in Hawaii smile at me because I was just a mere human being!

It is important that I begin this discussion on "English-Only" in Hawaii because it is there that I carelessly made one of my biggest blunders pertaining to language study/acquisition. I lived in Hawaii for over twenty-five years before moving to the U.S. mainland. I married a haole girl from Garden Grove, California there. Our three children were born there. Now if you were to ask me how much of the Hawaiian language I learned there, the beautiful language of a beautiful, sovereign people – I would sheepishly have to say, "Well, I learned three words; "aloha," "aloha," and "aloha." Yes, I learned three words, all which separately mean "hello," "good-bye," and "love." How terribly sad! And here I was – a teacher, even had a college masters degree by then.

Later when I took some classes in the process to receive an endorsement in "English as Second Language" (ESL) at Arizona State, I recall one of the instructors mentioning that sometimes we treat the languages other than the primary one as "marked languages." A "marked language" is one used by many in a particular culture, but not considered important, or worthy to the dominant culture. The dominant culture is not necessarily the most populace. Guess which are the most dominant? At this moment, I feel that I should apologize to the native peoples of Hawaii for not considering their beautiful culture worthy of my participation, and also deeply regret not placing value and esteem on the deepest forms of aloha offered my family and me. **Mahalo, dear ones.**

"American-English"

American English is a very rich language, perhaps one of the richest on earth, though perhaps in my opinion one of the least sonorous of the major ones. (The quick-silver sounds of Portuguese and French are awesome.) English is rich because as the nation it represents, it is also highly imperialistic. Please "bear" or is it "bare" with me? I love these American idioms. American-English, of course, is based on the mother tongue of England, which in spite of picking up a few Native words here and there, tried to annihilate (notice **it did not assimilate** into the local Native sounds, like the "dominants" want everyone else to do now) most of the indigenous languages. You will notice that I do not use that mythical word "Indian" to refer to the local original "Americans;" to me the Indian folk are either in India or working all night at the 7-11s (bless their hearts). I do wish we would, in English, rid ourselves once and for all of this American Indian stuff. And, in this same vein/vane return all of the beautiful Native (The Peoples of the Flesh) names to their "rightful" owners; names like "Strong Face in the Water," or "Hair of Turquoise Corn," instead of the Anglo "uncle" Tom Caine or Helen Haynes. Some of us that are able should dis-assimilate into our original names, names that once had a personal characteristic meaning or a strong connecting word to a thing, history, place, or an action.

American English is like a giant amoeba, slowly creeping along here and there, snacking on any host while making it its own. As stated before, originally our English came from "Great" Britain with its beautiful King James and Shakespearean modulations, bringing along many French words (French law terms, etc), and obscure Latin contributions. While here in "America" it acquired many Spanish words like tacos, salsa, tornado, corral, ranch, hacienda, adiós, etc. Unfortunately it did not acquire the correct pronunciation for some words like llama (yama) for llama (incorrect "lama" – no such animal in Peru), or amarillo, like the town in Texas (amariyo, meaning yellow, for a reason. Every time I hear the Anglo pronunciation of "guerrilla" as "gorilla" (should be guerriya, "lone" warrior), I envision gorillas with helmets and combat boots trudging through the jungle looking for bananas. Get it by now? An "ll" makes a beginning "y" sound. And since nobody has ever told you before, h's are silent in Spanish like in some English words like honor – hence no Hernandez, but 'Ernandez. No big deal, but if Anglos want everyone else to speak the English correctly, they should learn other languages correctly as well. Sometimes I strongly desire that Caucasians see how they seem to others – like a Mr. Magoo (he conjures in his mind what he desires to see, names it, it then "becomes" what he named it – just like the actions of a blind king). Non-Spanish-speaking people should pronounce Spanish words correctly, not as a legalistic type commandment, but as a way to **show respect** for another's language and culture. And native speakers should gently teach and encourage "proper" use of their language. Two-way street?

The English amoeba continued into the Pacific, into places like Havaii (aloha, hula, poi, lei, luau, ukulele (jumping flee); the Philippines (run amok, 'go crazy'); and Japan (sumu, geisha, kamikaze, hara-kiri, samurai, tsunami, kimono, and sushi; by the way, sushi is a roll of dry rice with fish or other meat inside. It does not mean "raw fish." Tell Mr. Magoo that the correct word for raw fish is "sashimi." Also by the wayside, the original Mr. Magoo was Christopher Columbus: "Yes, we have reached India; those half-naked savages must be Indians (indios)."

Myth – "Official-English" as the "American Unifier"

Before I comment on this, I must tell you of a memory I just had. Many years ago, when I was a younger man, I visited the City of New York. As I walked down one of the avenues, I heard all sorts of languages being spoken by many diverse-looking people. Some people were dressed in saris, some had big rags on their heads, some had little cup-cake hats, some had regular three-piece suits. I thought to myself, "How cool!" Maybe then it was more like, "Far out!" I literally thought, "I can be yelling out loud in made-up gibberish and nobody would pay any attention to me." I now wonder, "Why would this experience be thrilling to me, whereas to someone else, they might feel threatened and think, "This is America! Why aren't they speaking English!" I do not know the answer. I just know that it would have been quite boring if everyone had dressed the same and spoke just one language. Would I want them to be able to speak to each other and me with them? Admittedly yes, to a certain extent. If we could not communicate verbally, I know that a certain sensitivity would "kick in," and if it was truly important, we would find a way to "reach" into each other (and if we didn't, both of our lives "would go on" in peace.)

I think that my next comment may be one of the most intriguing to refute that "English" is going to **unify** the U.S. **We all recall that America once had a brutal and uncivilized civil war. What language did the South speak? English. What language did the North speak? English. Did the common language unify the Nation? No and no and no. In the end, what brought everyone together was sensitivity to the truth and the well-being of all men, with Liberty and Justice for All. Is it going to be any different in today's schisms?**

Spanish Also

Let's do a little experiment. I would like you to imagine something. Close your eyes. Now in your mind begin to see the names of places with Spanish names, all the way from Florida to California. Do you see names and places like: States: <u>Colorado</u> ("Colored Red"), <u>Nevada</u>

("Snowcapped [sierra]"), New Mexico (Calqued from *Nuevo México*), Montana (from *Montaña*: "Mountain"), and California (from the name of an imaginary island in "Las Sergas de Esplandián", a popular Spanish chivalry novel of the time/*Cali* from Caliente [meaning hot], *Forn* from Forno [meaning stove in Medieval Spanish], *ia* giving the land a female name); Florida (flowered); Arizona (from *Zona arida*: "Arid zone").

- Territories: Puerto Rico (means "Rich Port" in Spanish, reflecting the colonial mindset focused on gold and seafaring), Northern Mariana Islands (Named after Mariana of Austria; once a consort queen of Spain); U.S. Virgin Islands from *Islas Vírgenes*)

- Cities: Fresno ("Ash Tree"), Las Vegas ("The fertile lowlands"), Los Ángeles ("The angels", a shortened version of the original name Nuestra Señora Reina de los Ángeles "Our Lady Queen of Angels"), Modesto ("Modest"), Palo Alto ("Tall Cane"), San Francisco ("Saint Francis"), Amarillo ("Yellow"), Boca Ratón (from *Boca Ratón*: "Mouth of the River Mouse"), El Paso, Texas ("The Pass"), San Diego ("Saint James"), San José ("Saint Joseph"), Santa Clara ("Saint Claire"), Santa Rosa ("Saint Rose"), Santa Ana ("Saint Anne"), San Bernardino ("Saint Bernard"), San Antonio ("Saint Anthony"), Sacramento ("Sacrament"), Santa Fé (from "Santa Fé": Holy Faith), Corte Madera ("Cut Wood") etc.

- Regions: Llano Estacado ("Staked Plain"), Cape Canaveral (Anglicized from *Cabo Cañaveral*), Sierra Nevada ("Snowy Mountains"), etc.

- Islands: <u>Alcatraz</u> (from: *Alcatraz* "<u>Gannet</u>"), <u>Farallon Islands</u> (from: *Farallones* "High Cliffs"), <u>Alameda</u> ("Poplar Grove"), <u>Key West</u> (Anglicized from *Cayo Hueso*: "Bone Cay"), <u>Key Largo</u> (from Hollywood: the present place name was never given by the Spanish but adopted after the Bogart film, Key largo; "Long Key" is a separate islet in the chain, however Matecumbe and Isla Morada are original Spanish place names in the "Keys" or 'Cayos').

- Streets and Roads: <u>El Camino Real</u> ("The Royal Road" or "The King's Highway"), <u>Santa Monica Boulevard</u> (from *Santa Mónica*: "Saint Mónica"), <u>San Pablo Avenue</u> ("St. Paul"), Avenida de las Pulgas ("Avenue of the Fleas"), Camino Pablo ("Path of [Saint] Paul"), etc.

Imagine that for each place with a Spanish name that you remembered and thousands of others, including street names, that you didn't know, there once stood a Hispanic person naming it for his culture. (Why are there hardly, if any, African names in our American places. **Because the white owners killed the native languages of the slaves?** Yes, boss? I think that if I was black, I would change my name to one with an African connection, be rid of the slave owners' names.) In continuing with the Spanish language, can you imagine a bit further? Every place with a Spanish name was also actually "owned" by a Spanish speaker until they were forced to give it up at the point of a gringo pistola. True or false? **To date, every Spanish name still protests the thievery.** (Though indeed, without deed, the properties were first "owned" by the Native Americans.) I am trying to present this viewpoint so that these "<u>English

Only" personas will get some idea that the U.S. was not and is not just one White-English-Speaking-Nation-Under-God; as if God is only in America, blesses only America.

You know that we spend millions of dollars in our schools for our children to have a well-rounded education, part of this being to learn foreign languages. We think that by learning a foreign language we will teach our students to learn to communicate with others in another language, learn about their culture, learn to appreciate each other's differences. Español is the most widely taught non-English language in U.S. secondary schools and institutions of higher education, indicating its importance among non-Hispanic Americans. But then in our most perverse minds, we politicos want to limit and even abolish its use in public! Ay caramba!

Spanish is the second most common language in the United States after English. There are more Spanish speakers in the United States than there are speakers of French (another language inherited from European colonization), Hawaiian, and the various Native American languages taken all together. According to the 2000 United States Census, Spanish is spoken most frequently at home by about 28.1 million people aged 5 or over. Of these, 14.3 million reported that they also spoke English "very well". The United States is home to more than 40 million Hispanics, making it the fifth largest Spanish-speaking community in the world, after Mexico, Colombia, Spain, and Argentina.

New Mexico is commonly thought to have Spanish as an official language alongside English, due to the widespread usage of Spanish in the state. In fact, although the original state constitution of 1912 provided for a temporarily bilingual government, New Mexico has no official language. Although Spanish is not the most spoken language in any one U.S. state, it is the second most spoken language in 43 states and in the District of Columbia.

Over 1.4 million college students were enrolled in language courses in Fall 2002 and Spanish is the most widely taught language at American colleges with 53% of total people enrolled, followed by French (14.4%), German (7.1%) and Italian at (4.5%), although their total numbers remain relatively small of total population.

Speakers of Spanish in the United States
1. New Mexico (823,352) 43.27%
2. California (12,442,626) 34.72%
3. Texas (7,781,211) 34.63%
4. Arizona (1,608,698) 28.03%
5. Nevada (531,929) 22.80%
6. Colorado (878,803) 19.10%
7. Florida (3,304,832) 19.01%
8. New York (3,076,697) 15.96%
9. New Jersey (1,294,422) 14.90%
10. Illinois (1,774,551) 13.94%
11. Connecticut (371,818) 10.63%
12. Utah (253,073) 10.45%
13. Rhode Island (111,823) 10.35%
14. Oregon (343,278) 9.56%
15. Idaho (123,900) 8.88%
16. District of Columbia (47,258) 8.53%
17. Washington (526,667) 8.48%

18. <u>Kansas</u> (220,288) 8.06%

Although the state does not have an official language, laws in New Mexico are promulgated in Spanish as well as English, although English is the working language of the state government. Spanish has been spoken around northern New Mexico, southern Colorado and the U.S.-Mexican border since the 16th century. The range of Spanish rule in the late 18th and early 19th centuries encompassed much of the present-day US territory, including the French colony of Louisiana briefly under the Spanish from 1763 to 1800 and part of the US since 1803.

In Texas, English is conventionally used in government, but the state has no official language. Texas inherited a large Tejano population after the Mexican-America War. In addition, a steady influx of Spanish-speaking immigrants increased the import of Spanish in Texas. Even in the 21st century, southernmost counties of Texas in the Rio Grande Valley are mostly Latino, and Spanish is a common language among the region's multi-generational Mexican-Americans, but are more English-proficient than their southern neighbors.

Spanish is the first language of Puerto Rico, whose citizens hold statutory U.S. citizenship. Many Puerto Ricans have migrated to New York City, New York, adding to the Spanish-speaking population there. However, millions of Puerto Rican Americans that live across the U.S. mainland, also have fluency in the Spanish language. In Hawaii, where Puerto Rican farm laborers and Mexican ranchers settled since the late

1800s, 7 percent of the islands' people are Hispanic and also are Spanish-speakers.

Another Myth- (Don't speak your native tongue at home) "My child, at home speak English only! Do not speak our language and that of our ancestors. It will only make you un-American and you will not succeed in your studies, your career, your life, your entire upward mobility." Bull Ca-ca. I can safely bet all of the marbles in the jars of my childhood, that 99.9% of those who had parents that spoke a language other than English at home, wish that they would have learned the "foreign" language from them and as such would have immensely enriched their adult lives. I treasure the three languages that I speak, the two I understand.

Forms/Signs/Voting Ballots

"Why should I have to pay for all these extra forms, signs, and voting ballots in all these other God-forsaken tongues?" This is a question asked by many of our Anglo citizenry. Yes, why should the forms be in languages other than English (Spanish, Chinese, Tagalog)? Well, first of all these other languages are "legal tender" in communication between thousands, even millions, of humans who deserve equal representation in our republican nation, especially since they are paying for this service in payment of their taxes, whether they be in the forms of sales, income, or many of the other taxes stamped on our foreheads. The Vietnamese-American, the Chinese-American, the Mexican-American don't ever say at the grocer's counter, "Oh, sorry. Prease do not charge me the tax, I am not a White-American." But they do indeed pay their taxes and thus deserve services, especially in their own language. This then insures their rights of life, liberty, and the pursuit of happiness guaranteed in the Declaration of Independence for all its citizens, regardless of what language they choose to speak. So, if they paid **"taxes without representation,"** they would not be getting an equitable arrangement. I believe that a certain country was once at war in **1776** because of this particular unjust matter.

Press "One" for English, "Dos" for Español

Nothing seems to "irk" or should it be a little stronger, "pisses off" an English speaker more than to have to hear the English or Spanish selection on the start of a phone call. And nobody gets more irked than Tom Tancredo, our presidential candidate from the state with the Spanish name of Colorado. He says that he will not cease his quixotic-like crusade on illegal immigration and his stand on Official English, until he no longer hears those infernal words, "Press English one, Spanish two. (I wonder what he does in the grocery store when he is asked, "Señor, papel o plastic?") I believe that our phone selections should be, "Press One for English Only, Two if you are a Bigot, Press KKK if you are a Racist, and if all of the above, Press 666." LOL. Mr. Tancredo, I think he said this (reason why I am not a scholar), also believes that any child born in the U.S. to "illegals" should not become an American citizen automatically, as has been such a right for generations (Constitutional?). Sounds like somebody again is ostracizing a particular race, as I mentioned previously was once done to my other ancestors, the Chinese. And Mr. Tancredo wonders why people surmise that he overuses the KKK button on his telephone? I must add this in. I just saw Mr. Tancredo in all his wizardry on C-

Span. He was stomping the small Iowa town halls for possible future votes. Again, as he played his usual role as Don Quijote de la Mancha (tipping all those windmill dragons), he expounded on the dangers of the encroaching Spanish language. He continued to spit out his vociferous warnings when, walaah! - He dramatically pulled out a copy of a small town Iowan newspaper from underneath his suit coat. "Ladies and gentlemen," he craftily began. "This is a nearby local newspaper, not one from a town near the U.S.-Mexican border. Notice it has headlines both in English and Spanish!" The audience gasped! It was as if they had just read the mass murder headlines of some of their kinfolk. Part of me wanted to laugh and the other part felt like dry upchucking. Heaven help us. Since Mr. T. seems to hate things foreign so much, perhaps he should spend more of his time starting an initiative that would change the name of the State of Colorado (a Spanish word) to Red! Mr. Tancredo, I know you have a heart, but tell me, in your "heart of hearts," if these immigrants (documented or undocumented) were of white skin, (not sun-browned by toil), of blond hair, blue eyes, and spoke Italiano, would you still be hounding them, showing them your vitriolic fangs? I am almost certain that you and most of us for a fact, would not allow such people to be banded like chickens and spread out shoeless on hot cement sidewalks.

It seems quite disheartening that the "English One, Spanish Two" phone situation has such a negative and emotional response (being "irked") on some people. I see this more as capitalists trying to capitalize on a buck, and of others having a complete understanding of what a conversation is supposed to do: have honest and clear communication. Why must we have government legislate our speech because some (a lot of) individuals are control freaks (They want you to "Be just like me!") and/or are fearful of and threatened by things "foreign" (xenophobic)? It is truly "much ado about nothing," or of "much darkness of the heart." Only we can decide. In the end, it is not a question of English versus Spanish, but of human decency. And as such, should we allow nativist fears to detour the heart-felt dreams of such noble teachers as Mahatma Gandhi, Martin Luther King Jr., and Mother Theresa? It is only humane for each one of us to dream of a world in which equal opportunity is granted to all, equal resources available to all, and equal dignity is accorded to all, so that all may experience equally the unequaled wonder of Life.

"English-Only" vs. "Constitutional Freedom of Speech"

Consider the First Amendment of the Constitution of the United States: **"Congress shall make no law … abridging the freedom of speech or of the press."**

Without Freedom of Thought, there can be no such thing as Wisdom; to legislate Language one impairs Thought, Wisdom. There cannot be Freedom of Speech without the Freedom of Thought; to favor one Language, also to legislate such, is to prefer only one thought, an English one. In this Democracy not all thoughts are in one exclusive language (Chinatown, reservations, the Southwest); to deem so deprives many of a sacred privilege so essential to a democratic free government. Freedom of Speech is the great Defender of Liberty; they shall either prosper or die together.
In any country where a Man cannot call his Tongue his own, he can scarcely call anything, his own. The

minds of men call for Equality, which is the soul of Liberty, and those minds must be afforded great utterance either in voice or written expression. It is the right of every man to succeed in his own free voice without the betrayal of government. Where there is no Liberty of Speech and/or Language, there is only deprivation and punishment; hardly an abode for Life, Liberty, and the Pursuit of Happiness. To oppress a language is to commence the extinction of a RACE, CULTURE, SELF; thus the legislation of English as the (only) official language of a United States shall prove to be Unconstitutional.

(If you lose the Language, You lose the Culture)

"NATIVE TONGUE"

When I Dream about running with the deer
Through the stone monuments in the valleys…
I use my Native Tongue.
When I teach my children the
Wisdom of the Ancestors…
I use may Native Tongue.

When I Love my woman dearly…
I use the Native Tongue
of the Sacred Animals.

Once, when the foreigners came,
They took our lands,
Put us in reservations without menus,
Spit on us …
With their snaking forked tongues.
Once, to protect us from our
"Pagan" Native Tongues
They stole our children,
Put them in caged boarding houses,

Made them deaf and mute - alone.
They taught them a religion about love, Yet
Without the true love of the Great Spirit.

Now they wish to annihilate
our Dreams, Our Wisdom,
our Loving -
With their foolish tongue
of English-Only.

Bilingualism

Bilingualism in Canada– Official <u>Bilingualism</u> in <u>Canada</u> refers to laws and policies that make English and French the official languages in Canada, mandating that the federal government – and some other levels of government – provide certain services and communication to the public in both <u>English</u> and <u>French</u>.

Official languages are addressed in the <u>Canadian Charter of Rights and Freedoms</u> (sections 16 to 23), in the <u>Official Languages Act</u>, and <u>Official Language Regulations</u>. These laws establish the equality of status of English and French in federal institutions and guarantee the rights of English or French linguistic minorities in Canada.

The population of the country itself is by a large majority <u>monolingual</u> as only 17.65% of Canadians can speak both English and French. The bilingual policies of the government are controversial to many, especially to those who support the <u>Quebec sovereignty movement</u>, and to many <u>conservatives</u>.

Support for bilingualism in Canada is mixed. Some, mostly English-speaking Canadians living in provinces with small French populations, resent the federal bilingualism policies as unnecessary and excessive government regulation, and for those opponents, the presence of French on Canadian products and road signs is a constant reminder of the policy. Many French-speaking Canadians in Quebec, though benefiting from the inclusive labeling law, resent the federal bilingualism policies just as strongly, seeing them as an attempt to dilute their language and culture with English. Quebec's <u>Anglophone community</u>, like their Francophone counterparts throughout English Canada, tend to be "for" rather than "against" the policy. Support for bilingualism appears to be strongest in the area known as the <u>bilingual belt</u>, covering parts of Ontario, Manitoba, western Quebec and Montreal, and the areas of the <u>Maritimes</u>, and weakest in western Canada, though there are supporters and opponents in every part of the country.

I begin with Canadian Bilingualism so that there would be no continuing hu-hu (Hawaiian for "crying" (I did learn more than three words in Hawaiian]) from the "English-Only" contingency. There are other English-speaking countries that have had to deal with multiple language issues as well as the U.S. These countries even made their **country bilingual**, "heaven forbid" that would happen here. Maybe next year. Send shivers up and down that Hispanophobic spine? (By the way, two languages, not one, are spoken by whites in South Africa, English and Afrikaans).

Immersion – "Bilingual Education is costly, wasteful and ineffectual and non-English speaking students, mainly Hispanics, don't learn a lick of English in bilingual classes," bemoans the ignorance of a new-clouded age. (Again, don't forget that some taxes of color should go to services of colour [no taxation without representation].) I could admit to "Immersion Only" being a successful method of language instruction if you were a mature adult and were only required to understand, speak, and write the targeted language. I feel it is a different situation when one is a young person trying to "learn" a language plus much of the **content matter**, such as science, history, social studies, math, etc. Bilingual classes teach these subjects in whatever language is most beneficial at the time, with the knowledge that learning English is definitely a goal, but not the only desired outcome. I would even include the teaching of reading and writing in their primary language. Many "foreign" students have not even attained these skills, having been ill-schooled or not schooled at all in their previous country. It has been established that children who read and write in their native language transfer this knowledge to written English, thus accelerating their progress in literacy and academic content learning. In my view, if you are indeed highly "educated" in any language, you will be successful in some endeavor, for your education will lead you; just because one speaks English does not automatically guarantee success. Our own American students take "English" for twelve years in school, and I dare say that as adults, most cannot even write a one-page article successfully.

In 1988, English-Only proponents in California were able to slash funding for bilingual education programs. These groups boasted that students would learn English in a year in an English-Only Immersion class. But four years later, they discovered that this approach had failed miserably. Less than half of non-English speaking students enrolled in English Immersion programs had attained proficiency in English, and there was no tangible evidence that English Immersion programs improved English skills of students faster or more effectively than students in bilingual education courses. Believe me, since I have observed it, young limited English students in an English-Only class appear as a body that cannot hear, cannot talk, almost cannot even see, for though it can still breathe, it is a life that is no longer there. The only thing that lives in its place is an abundance of this stabbing emotion: daily frustration.

The failure of the English-Only approach to deliver new generations of proficient English speaking students was no surprise. A decade earlier, a federal study to determine whether bilingual education helped or hindered the attainment of English proficiency concluded that bilingual education was not the losing proposition that English-Only advocates claimed. It found that well-funded and implemented programs enabled Limited English speaking students to catch up to their English fluent classmates at a faster rate. It also found that it took students nearly five years to fully master English, and not the one year that English Only backers claimed an Immersion program would take. At this point I'd like to mention two positive observations I had a pleasure to witness. The first is that I found the bilingual teachers (most were bilingual themselves, spoke the students' language) a most compassionate lot. They truly believe that what they are doing will help their students tremendously, in fact, possibly save their lives. The latter is important for they realize the sort of dangerous neighborhood (barrio) their students come from and that a good education, whether in English or Spanish, will be of paramount importance in lifting themselves up to a better future.

The second terrific occurrence I experienced in a bilingual class was when I saw a young white, blond, blue-eyed, third-grader speaking flawless and fluent Spanish as she did her lessons. Of all the students in the class, be they white, black, brown, I'd certainly pick her to have the most extraordinary and successful adult life. I was extremely pleased and proud to have seen this for I felt I was witnessing the true spirit of bilingualism and of our country. It gave me hope for our country – if only we adults can steer our halting hearts smoothly in the right direction.

Language Sidebar – The LPGA tour, the leading tour in women's golf, stood accused of infringing the rights of many of its members after introducing a rule stipulating that players who cannot communicate in English will be suspended. This edict was principally directed at Korean golfers. As if Arnold Palmer and Jack Nicklaus had to accept their trophies in foreign languages when they won in foreign lands.

~~~~~~

"I am a builder and I ONLY hire people from south of the border anymore. I used to be able to hire American boys but not anymore they, don't seem to want to work. I pay my men well and pay bonuses for jobs well done and so they work enthusiastically. I have not known individuals more sincere and earnest in over 20 years. I employed one young man who walked all the way here from El Salvador to provide support for his sister so that she might finish high school. He lived in a one car garage, slept on a stack of pallets and paid rent for it. It was that important to him. I have employed countless men, young and old who have left their homes and families to obtain a better life for their loved ones. Imagine, if you can, yes YOU, needing to leave your family, your wife and sons and daughters, in order to provide a better life for them. Imagine facing the necessity to move to a country where you do not speak the language in the hopes of providing a better life for your family. Imagine having no choice. My mother's parents were Italian immigrants and no, they didn't speak English all that well but they worked their hearts out and provided for their children which, in turn, provided for me. I was blessed, as were you all. You largely seem to have forgotten your roots. One of my employees has two children who were born here. I asked my attorney who specializes in immigration how I could get my helper and his wife legal since their two sons were naturalized citizens and I was told that if I tried to do that the parents would be sent back to Mexico and the children put into foster care... And this from "Christians".. family values?.. in a pigs eye.... and so they continue to live "under the radar". And so, my helper continues to build your homes and his wife continues to clean your homes. They are no different than the Irish, the Italian, the German, the Polish or any other nationality that has emigrated here in the hopes of making a better life for their loved ones with the exception of the fact that our government has made it impossible for these new immigrants to obtain legal status here. Your grandparents faced no such obstacles. I refer those of you who take exception to my point of view to Corinthians 13." by Bruce DeLacey | 12:49 PM | 9-7-2008

Part VI.
Amnesty, Costs, Social Security
Maquiladoras, NAFTA, Assimilation

"Justice vs. Law" - 24"x 36"

The Cost of Illegal Immigration

We all would agree that the education of our children and our citizenry should be one of the most important tasks for our government to embark upon. Yes, we all say and assume this, but yet when the time comes to adequately fund educational programs, we fail horribly. Our perspective and/or priorities become third-hand whims. For example, the budget for NASA is $17,000,000,000 per year. NASA hopes to find aliens on Mars, which we shall quickly place behind a wire fence. It hopes to find water, which we shall immediately pollute. I am not trying to berate the endeavors of space exploration, but when our children in inner city schools have no school supplies, where teachers use their own funds in order to make their programs function (the government knows all about this for it gives teachers miniscule tax credits). I believe that **public funds** should be spent on funding programs for the public. The space programs always seem to me as a picture of a dad driving around in his nice new Cadillac or Jaguar while his children do not have any chews or shoes. Misappropriated priorities and funds?

The war in Iraq is costing 200 million dollars per day, 6 billion per month. Isn't that enough money to finance quality educational programs, a universal health care system? I wish that the twenty or so B-2 stealth bombers (cost- 2.2 billion each!) that we have, stealthfully flying around from air show to air show would be so stealth as to quietly disappear out of our budgets, leave a trail of folded origami dollars for our depressed city children to turn into paper, pencils, and crayons as they somersault laughingly into their fruitful futures. But not likely?

Our inner cities are a disgrace. Besides having high crime rates, run-down down buildings badly in need of repair, hope is sadly run down also. It would take an armed guard such as found in Iraq for us outsiders to safely walk down the streets even in broad daylight. Guns, guns everywhere. More than Baghdad?

Weapons of Mass Destruction

By the way, have you heard the latest? The **WMDs** (weapons of mass destruction) were not found to be in Iraq, but found everywhere else around the world, found in **hunger, homelessness, and illiteracy**, and much closer to home than anyone had imagined. The weapons of mass destruction are all around us, but we see only what we desire to see. **We would rather be arguing about what official language to make out the death certificates of those that have just died, entered into the Fourth World from the Third World.** The Fourth World is the immediate world of death, where thousands of people have just entered – they died of starvation while you read this.

I sometimes wonder if those starving black African children with flies for eyes, bloated watermelon stomachs (full of worms), and stick-figure arms and legs – **As Seen On TV** – had they been a shade of white, would they have been already fed and tucked in our American beds by now? I'm talking about me here?

In Chile, the fishermen sell their fish to American pet companies, rather than to the poor of their country, because they can get more money for it. Imagine, our pets in the U.S. have their own department stores (such as Pet Smart) where they can use their own debit/credit cards? And yip, yip, yips from little Chihuahua dogs have more power than cries from the malnourished orphans of Chihuahua.

In the U.S., we have hot dog eating contests where the winner can eat 66 hotdogs in 12 minutes; we have future brides in their wedding gowns trying to "outdo" each other by stuffing themselves with wedding cake, as the children in The Fourth World watch from their graves. Should anyone play games with food?

The current (Bush) administration deludes itself in proudly stating that it has rid our country of "hunger"… by now calling it, **"severe food deprivation!"** Ay!

Economic Effects

Opinions vary about the economic effects of immigration. Those who find that immigrants produce a negative effect on the U.S. economy often focus on the difference between taxes paid and government services received and wage-lowering effects among low-skilled native workers, while those who find positive economic effects focus on added productivity and lower costs to consumers for certain goods and services. In a late 1980s study, economists themselves overwhelmingly viewed immigration, including illegal immigration, as a positive for the economy. According to James Smith, a senior economist at Santa Monica-based RAND Corporation and lead author of the United States National Research Council's study "The New Americans: Economic, Demographic, and Fiscal Effects of Immigration," immigrants contribute as much as $10 billion to the U.S. economy each year. The NRC report found that although immigrants, especially those from Latin

America, were a net cost in terms of taxes paid versus social services received, overall immigration was a net economic gain due to an increase in pay for higher-skilled workers, lower prices for goods and services produced by immigrant labor, and more efficiency and lower wages for some owners of capital. The report also noted that although immigrant workers compete with domestic workers for some low skilled jobs, some immigrants specialize in activities that otherwise would not exist in an area, and thus are performing services that otherwise would not exist, and thus can be beneficial to all domestic residents. About 21 million immigrants, or about 15 percent of the labor force, hold jobs in the United States. However, the number of unemployed is only seven million, meaning that immigrant workers are not taking jobs from domestic workers. Rather, they are doing jobs that would not have existed had the immigrant workers not been in the United States. U.S. Census Bureau's *Survey of Business Owners: Hispanic-Owned Firms: 2002* indicated that the number of Hispanic-owned businesses in the United States grew to nearly 1.6 million in 2002. Those Hispanic-owned businesses generated about $222 billion in revenue. The report notes that the burden of poor immigrants is not born equally among states, and is most heavy in California. Another claim that those supporting current and expanded immigration levels is that immigrants mostly do jobs Americans don't want. A 2006 Pew Hispanic Center report added evidence to support that claim when they found that increasing immigration levels have not hurt employment prospects for American workers.

In 2009, a study by the Cato Institute, a free market think tank, found that legalization of low-skilled illegal resident workers in the US would result in a net increase in US GDP of $180 billion over ten years.

Jason Riley notes that "because of progressive income taxation, in which the top 1% of earners pay 37% of federal income taxes (even though they actually pay a lower tax percentage based on their income, which puts the majority of the national tax burden on the poor and middle class), 60% of Americans collect more in government services than they pay in." Thus, it is not remarkable that some immigrants would do the same. In any event, the typical immigrant and his children will pay a net $80,000 more in their lifetimes than they collect in government services, according to the NAS.

The Kauffman Foundation's index of entrepreneurial activity is nearly 40% higher for immigrants than for natives. Immigrants were involved in the founding of many prominent American high-tech companies, such as Google, Yahoo, Sun Microsystems, and eBay.

On the poor end of the spectrum, the **"New Americans"** report found that low-skill low wage immigration does not, on aggregate, lower the wages of most domestic workers. The report also addresses the question of if immigration affects black Americans differently from the population in general: "While some have suspected that blacks suffer disproportionately from the inflow of low-skilled immigrants, none of the available evidence suggests that they have been particularly hard-hit on a national level. Some have lost their jobs, especially in places where immigrants are concentrated. But the majority of blacks live elsewhere, and their economic fortunes are tied to other factors.

At the June 13, 1998, Commencement Address at Portland State University, President Bill Clinton said, "new immigrants are good for America. They are revitalizing our cities...building our new economy...strengthening our ties to the global economy, just as earlier waves of immigrants settled on the new frontier and powered the Industrial Revolution. They are energizing our culture and broadening our vision of the world. They are renewing our most basic values and reminding us all of what it truly means to be an American."

Foreign Aid – (Remit Money and Ideas)

It appears that this section ($$$) has many miscellaneous, chop-suey, entries. One last one shall be included; the complaint that throughout the centuries, many of the undocumented or documented immigrants have sent much money to relatives in their native lands and not having spent it in the U.S. **Could anyone think of a better form of Foreign Aid?** The U.S.A. does send millions of aid overseas. It goes in the form of dollars, grain, equipment, and unfortunately in military arms. It is no secret that this aid often never reaches those that need it the most. Too often it ends up in the deep pockets of dictators, crooked military leaders, corrupt politicians, and in the inefficiency of foreign beauracracies. When a migrant or an immigrant sends funds, which he earned with his hard sweat (not a handout), it goes directly to a family that usually desperately needs it. Without the workers' help, a painful situation would most certainly have occurred. In 2005, Mexicans in the United States remitted some $20 billion home, about 3 percent of Mexico's income. Remittances now exceed tourism, oil, and the maquiladoras (U.S. assembly plants inside of Mexico) as the country's top single source of foreign exchange. The billions of dollars that migrants send back each year help to start businesses, build roads, and even fund medical care. But according to journalist, Peggy Levitt in *"Life, Liberty, and the Folks Back Home,"* immigrants also send back social remittances: New ideas from America, and about America that are changing societies profoundly around the world. They talk about their experiences in the United States, overcoming ignorance and suspicion among people in the countries they come from. And immigrants, having seen what is possible, can be forceful, grass-roots advocates for change. When it comes to the debate about immigration, our focus on economics, and in particular the economic impact in the United States, is far too narrow. Ideas and values matter. Immigrants bring ideas to this country, making our society richer."

Immigrants and Social Security

Social commentator Michael Ennis, stated in one of his lectures:
"Recently retired Federal Reserve chairman Alan Greenspan recently observed that our large immigrant workforce has played an essential role restraining

inflation, by lowering the costs of basic goods and services, which itself cushions the shock to low-income Americans. That illegal immigrants are a net burden on the welfare system is also a popular belief, but the 1996 welfare reform bill excluded even legal immigrants from most federal assistance. Illegal immigrants pay billions each year in Social Security taxes for which they receive no benefits, and we often overlook the state and local sales taxes, fees, and property taxes (in the form of rent) they also pay. Many economists now forecast that in the long run, all those immigrants will compensate for the declining birthrate among the rest of us, not only taking up the slack as baby boomers retire but also playing an essential role in funding boomers' Social Security benefits."

Mexico's Economic Turmoil - Immigration to U.S.

Promises As economic conditions have led many Mexican workers to U.S. jobs that often support families back home, an estimated one in six Mexicans now lives in the United States. The past six years have brought increased instability to Mexican workers and labor markets which have led to contributing a sharp rise in immigration to the U.S., according to a new report by the Mexican Institute of Labor Studies. This study is the first detailed analysis of the economic performance of the administration of Vicente Fox who instituted policies that are being continued by President Felipe Calderon. The study, prepared by Professor Carlos Salas, says that Fox promised to improve the living conditions of Mexican workers and reduce migration of Mexicans to the U.S. However, none of those promises were realized. The report points out that growth of GDP per capita between 1994 and 2000 was 21.4%, while during the six years of the Fox administration it was only 7.9%. Mexico's trade figures improved, but only because of an accounting trick where foreign-produced inputs to maquiladoras are not calculated, but finished goods from maquiladoras are calculated as exports. Mexican exports to the U.S. have steadily decreased as the U.S. imports more from China. Many manufacturing plants that left the U.S. for Mexico under NAFTA have since left Mexico for China or other low-wage countries. The report says that Mexico is becoming increasingly dependent on remittances from Mexicans living in the U.S. Remittances also are the lifeblood of many rural communities and supplement that country's weak social safety nets. Given Mexico's slow growth and serious structural problems (poverty and inequality; corruption; low tax collections; poor education system; ineffective political checks and balances; inadequate infrastructure development; restrictive business regulations; rigid, antiquated, and inefficient labor market policies and institutions; and the limited capacities of governments at every level), it is unlikely that its citizens will have adequate job opportunities at home anytime soon.

Migration clearly is very important to Mexico: it provides a safety valve to compensate for that country's failure to provide adequate domestic jobs for most of its workforce growth, and remittances from the 20 to 25 million Mexicans living in the United States have become second only to oil exports as a source of Mexican foreign exchange. What the United States does about immigration, therefore, has important implications for Mexican economic and political developments, with significant positive or negative spillover effects for America. Now you know why most Presidents of Mexico don't attack the problem of immigration overly aggressive.

Maquiladoras

Most readers are knowledgeable about the maquiladaor system, but for those that are not, as I wasn't, the following is included:

A **maquiladora** or **maquila** is a factory that imports materials and equipment on a duty-free and tariff-free basis for assembly or manufacturing and then re-exports the assembled product, usually back to the originating country.

"Maquiladora" is primarily used to refer to factories in Mexican towns along the United States-Mexican border, but increasingly is used to refer to factories all over Latin America. Maquiladora factories encompass a variety of industries including electronics, transportation, textile, and machinery, among others. Maquiladoras may be 100% foreign-owned (usually by U.S. companies) in most countries. The use of maquiladoras is an example of off shoring. Other countries such as Japan, Germany, and Korea have maquiladoras as well, but the majority of them are located in Mexico and are associated with United States companies.

Maquiladoras originated in Mexico in the 1960s along the U.S. border. In the early to mid-1990s, there were approximately 2,000 maquiladoras with 500,000 workers. In just a few years, the number of plants has almost doubled and the number of workers has more than doubled. Maquiladoras primarily produce electronic equipment, clothing, plastics, furniture, appliances, and auto parts and today eighty percent of the goods produced in Mexico are shipped to the United States.

Competition from China has weakened the allure of maquiladoras in recent years and some report that more than 500 plants have closed since the beginning of the decade, causing a loss of several hundred thousand jobs. China is bolstering its status as the world's cheap assembly export location.

Since globalization has contributed to the competition and advent of low-cost offshore assembly in places like Taiwan, China, and other countries in Central America, maquiladoras in Mexico have been on the decline since 2000. According to federal sources, approximately 529 maquiladoras shut down, and investment in assembly plants decreased by 8.2 percent in 2002. Despite the decline, there still exist over 3,000 maquiladoras along the 2,000 mile-long United States-Mexican border, providing employment for approximately one million workers, and importing more than $51 billion in supplies into Mexico. As of 2006, maquiladoras still account for 45 percent of Mexico's exports.

Mexico possesses a strong system of labor laws, yet enforcement of these laws within the maquiladora industry is often lax. While most people who were employed under the original Bracero Program were men, the majority of maquiladora employees are women. Women are considered to be preferred to men because women will typically work for cheaper wages, and are easier for male employers to direct and impose poor working conditions on. Some maquiladora operators have admitted a preference for women also because women often display a greater level of patience and higher dexterity than men in performing the standardized and repetitive work of an assembly plant. Therefore, the maquila industry has, based on these conditions, been accused of the sexual exploitation of women. On the other hand, opponents of this allegation argue that women are paid higher wages working in a maquiladora than they commonly would in other forms of employment in northern Mexico. In addition, some have argued that maquiladora employment enables women to make their own money and thus become more independent, while teaching them new skills and giving them more opportunities that they may not otherwise acquire.

The maquiladora operators have also been accused of discrimination of child-bearing-aged women in order to keep costs down because Mexico's labor laws contain extensive maternity requirements. They often demand pregnancy tests as a prerequisite to employment or insist that female workers use birth control. If a woman is found to be pregnant, it may likely hinder her chances of getting hired, and if an existing worker becomes pregnant, she may be terminated.

In recent years, however, there has been a shift toward hiring more male workers due to labor shortages and the emergence of heavier industries operating within maquiladoras.

Low Wages, Long Hours

(It is disheartening to hear my fellow Americans cry out and complain that they have to live from paycheck to paycheck. They should feel blessed that they are getting one.)

One of the main goals of the maquiladora system was to attract foreign investment. In order to do that, Mexican labor must remain cheap and competitive with other major export countries to keep the United States firms operating within the Mexican assembly plants. So to keep production high and costs low, maquiladoras have been accused of harsh working environments, which include low wages, forced overtime, and illegal working conditions for minors. Mexican women work for approximately one-sixth of the U.S. hourly rate. It has also been reported that the income one receives from work in a maquiladora is rarely enough to support a family. Low wages are a main reason for foreign investment. However, some management personnel condone low wages in maquiladoras by arguing that the cost of living is lower in Mexico than in other countries. Employee turnover is also relatively high, reaching up to 80 percent in some maquiladoras, due in part to stress and health threats common to this type of labor.

Maquiladoras are owned by U.S., Japanese, and European countries and some could be considered "sweatshops" composed of young women working for as little as 50 cents an hour, for up to ten hours a day, six days a week. However, in recent years, NAFTA has started to pay off somewhat - some maquiladoras are improving conditions for their workers, along with wages.

Unfortunately, the cost of living in border towns is often 30% higher than in southern Mexico and many of the maquiladora women (many of whom are single) are forced to live in shantytowns that lack electricity and water surrounding the factory cities. Maquiladoras are quite prevalent in Mexican cities such as Tijuana, Ciudad Juarez, and Matamoros that lie directly across the border from the interstate highway-connected U.S. cities of San Diego (California), El Paso (Texas), and Brownsville (Texas), respectively.

The "Maquiladora system" included here again shows how the U.S. tries to "help" others economically, though all along heavily lining its own pockets. We have developed exploitation to a grand art.

In addition, the maquiladoras also exacerbated the problem of illegal immigration by luring those seeking work from the interior of Mexico to the border towns. Of course when they could neither find work there or could not stand the conditions at the maquiladoras, they just kept moving north to the U.S.

[There is space here so I'll place this simple comment about a particular ailment in Mexico. "Nothing gets done without the "Mordida" or "bite." Better translated yet as "Bribe." It is incredibly detrimental to a society, especially one that would claim itself a democracy, to realistically move forward economically and even socially in many instances without first eradicating this problem. In the early part of the twentieth century the U.S. had to "clean itself" up of this situation, along with the tempting practices of nepotism. In strong nation building, it is extremely important not to ignore this essential process.]

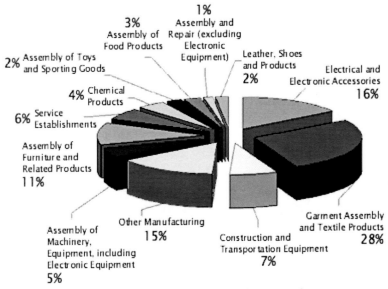

General sample activities that lure workers to the maquiladoras near the border.

Examples of Maquiladoras in Mexico

- 3 Day Blinds
- 20th Century Plastics
- Acer Peripherals
- Bali Company, Inc.
- Bayer Corp./Medsep
- BMW
- Canon Business Machines
- Casio Manufacturing
- Chrysler
- Daewoo
- Eastman Kodak/Verbatim
- Eberhard-Faber
- Eli Lilly Corporation
- Honda
- Honeywell, Inc.
- Hughes Aircraft
- Hyundai Precision America
- IBM
- Matsushita
- Mattel
- Maxell Corporation

- Ericsson
- Fisher Price
- Ford
- Foster Grant Corporation
- General Electric Company
- JVC
- GM
- Hasbro
- Hewlett Packard
- Hitachi Home Electronics
- Mercedes Benz
- Mitsubishi Electronics Corp.
- Motorola
- Nissan
- Philips
- Pioneer Speakers
- Samsonite Corporation
- Samsung
- Sanyo North America
- Sony Electronics
- Tiffany
- Toshiba
- VW
- Xerox
- Zenith

~~~~~~~~~~~~~~~~~~~

Water, Water, Water Everywhere?

Precious nectar that waters the Southwest, should be free to run downhill forever, but is often held hostage at the "border." The following is about El Río Grande, the 1885-mile river begins in Colorado, ends in Matamoros, Mexico. "Water on lips is a human right."

"Pilgrimage of Ghost Water"
I.
Awake! Arise! Pillowed Clouds from the deepest Pacific, Most southern Gulf.

Impregnate yourselves with life,
Carry your moistened child, Break your water,
Deliver it in a furious Stormy birth over the
awaiting mountains –
Where the two sisters, the San Juans,
The Bloody Range of Christ abide.

Let the diatoms of vanilla shaved ice lightly float.
Listen as the heavy hail carves itself deeply into
basalt Stones,
Watch the passing virga of veiled rain
Hide the alchemist turning a golden mist into
snow, Snow that streams as transparent milk,
Flows in tips of fingers to suckle a sandy valley
below.

II.

The rushing Upper Río Bravo runs by the
beaver's ear.
It is a fact the trickling and tickling sound
Is the age-old trigger that sends
The beaver into a shiver, quiver of all its parts –
Must dam the noise, Create a silence to a drip.
The man as a beaver also dreams the river,
Hears the speedboat, Minus the elk,
Hears the ski, Not on snow but on water,
Hears the whirring of the buzz-bait fishing lure
Minus a silent desert created,
Hears the picnic table
Full of laughter.

Awakened.
The beaverman hears
The jingle of soft money in his wide pockets –
Must dam the Canyon,
Fill it with his pleasures,

Must damn the future, the unknown.

III.

The old river was once young –
More full than foolish.
It had enough strength to water
The papas, the melgares, the Native Peoples of
Flesh.
It too had dreams –
It thought it could cool the long rooted toes
Of its friends the Alamos forever.

It loved to see the Night catfish
Playing in the trees,
Showing off their Cheshire smiles,
Curling their cattails with lighted candles.

It loved to play the Role
Of a long, long giving water snake
As it traveled to the South –
Where children could drink
Of it with whistling straws of hollow grass,
Where watering pots would fill themselves to
overflow,
Hold daily Life for man, his tamed beasts,
Where acequias would rush to fill the pores of
piñon, beans, and squash
To those faraway…faraway…still much afraid of
water snakes.

But that was forever, when it was young –
More full than foolish.
Now it was old, aged in slender –
Made to feel tired and empty
As it was nearly sucked dry of all its lifeblood

By overnight births of new cities
with thirsty needs for lush putting greens,
show-off neighbor lawns. And

By the dam dreams of upstream beavermen.
And even though it had also been made sluggish,
slow By leap-frogging water compacts
And Buttes of Elephants crying out for "More!"
It still had enough life to hatch Chile Verde
In the fertile beds of old Nuevo Méjico.

But then yet barely enough –
For as a bear waits for a salmon to return to its
birth, A Chocolate child of Ancient Aztec Corn
also waits, seeds in hand –
Waits for the clouds to return in a Godly
promise, In a new form, a streaming, gushing
water flow. But then as tomorrow –
Only tears water the cracked earth, As she spits,
curses El Norte.

"Cyclists Upstream" 24"x36"

NAFTA

The **North American Free Trade Agreement** is the trade bloc in North America created by the North American Free Trade Agreement (NAFTA) and its two supplements, the North American Agreement on Environmental Cooperation (NAAEC) and The North American Agreement on Labor Cooperation (NAALC), whose members are Canada, Mexico, and the United States. It came into effect on January 1, 1994.

The North American Free Trade Agreement NAFTA called off the majority of tariffs between products traded among the United States, Canada and Mexico, and gradually phased out other tariffs over a 15-year period. Restrictions were to be removed from many categories, including motor vehicles, computers, textiles, and agriculture. The treaty also protected intellectual property rights (patents, copyrights, and trademarks), and outlined the removal of investment restrictions among the three countries. The agreement is trilateral in nature (that is, the stipulations apply equally to all three countries) in all areas except agriculture, in which stipulation, tariff reduction phase-out periods and protection of selected industries, were negotiated bilaterally.

Since the advent of the lopsided, so-called free trade agreement, where U.S. corn and bean producers get to keep their government subsidies while poor and modest Mexican Indian farmers lose theirs, the bottom has fallen out of the regional and local farming villages. While these Indian villages have always experienced poverty, most have been self-sufficient, at least in producing and providing and sustaining from the basic Indian foods of corn, beans and other produce, chicken and pigs, the occasional cattle. That's the traditional Indian homestead for most of southern Mexico, Guatemala and elsewhere among agricultural communities in Mesoamerica and South America. This is the stalwart bastion of the mostly self-sufficient safety net upon which the people have depended for millennia. Indian people, real Mexican Indians - Maya, Zapoteca and other indigenous peoples, with distinct languages and varieties of ethnicity and oral tradition - have been severely displaced and dislocated over the past decade U.S. trade policies have a lot to do with it." "These are the bulk of the millions of new migrants inexorably making their way north. These are the Indian refugees displaced from their lands by the destruction of the old ejido systems, the privatization of water and lands, and the demolishment of a national economy that, up to 10 years ago, could make sense of the ancient Indian agricultural and gastronomic complex of the corn tortilla and the bean, grown and consumed locally and regionally.

Assimilation

"America the Beautiful" ranges from the Seminoles in the Southeast, the Inuit in the Far, Far Northwest, the Yankees in the Northeast, to the Yaquis in the Southwest. Why would anyone want to blend all of these wonderful cultures into a wigged, face-powdered, slave-owning George Washington?

There are those who would want to make the U.S. one race, one language, and one white history; unfortunately for them we are truly a nation of many races, languages, one over-all history, and many diverse cultures. Am I describing a multi-cultural nation? Many resent this fact, but cannot escape the reality.

Realties are only valid if they speak in truths. Is ketchup better than salsa; white bread better than tortillas; coat and a tie better than a serape or a poncho; a waltz better than a cha-cha; a Budweiser better than a Corona; a hamburger better than a taco; and English better than Spanish? Not really. It would be a bland America without either. When are we going to learn to "live and let live" and all join in the joyful dance of life?

We in America are not a "melting pot," but are more like participants in a great "**pot luck**," that fine and exquisite meal where each one brings their best-cooked recipe for all to taste, and **there is always plenty to go around**.

The following are comments by/of our All-American watchdog, **Patrick J. Buchanan** not unlike comments by racist Senator John C. Calhoun of the "All of Mexico" controversy in 1848:

"Immigration tsunami (What sort of word is tsunami, Pat?) will make whites a minority in US."
"The prognosis is grim. Between 2000 & 2050, world population will grow to over 9 billion people, but this 50% increase in global population will come entirely in Asia, Africa, & Latin America, as 100 million people of European stock vanish from the Earth. But the immigration tsunami rolling over America is not coming from 'all the races of Europe.' The largest population transfer in history is coming from all the races of Asia, Africa, and Latin America, and they are not 'melting' and reforming." Pat also warned in his xenophobic state, that the American Southwest could "become a giant

Kosovo", still part of the United States, but Mexican in "language, ethnicity, history and culture". In 1992, he said: "if we had to take a million immigrants in, say Zulus, next year, or Englishmen, and put them in Virginia, what group would be easier to assimilate and would cause less problems for the people of Virginia?" (How can Mr. Buchanan forget that the immigration situation would be based on a people's <u>need</u> and not their race?)

Buchanan says immigrants pose a potential security risk and that porous borders put America at risk for another terrorist attack. How about this as one of his zanier claims? "The Communist Chinese government has the secret loyalty of millions of 'overseas Chinese' from Singapore to San Francisco.", though he provides no evidence to support this accusation. <u>He also opposes Muslim immigration to the United States and Europe.</u>

In reading Mr. Buchanan's books it is clear that he expresses concern at the declining numbers of non-Hispanic whites in America, arguing that few nations have ever held together without an ethnic majority. In a 2002 speech, he said, "In the next 50 years, the Third World will grow by the equivalent of 30 to 40 new Mexicos. If you go to the end of the century, the white and European population is down to about three percent. This is what I call the death of the West. I see the nations dying when the populations die. I see the civilization dying. It is under attack in our own countries, from our own people." Buchanan believes that if these demographic trends continue, young Americans will spend their golden years in a "third world America", which will reduce the nation to a conglomeration of peoples with nothing in common. He believes this can be credited to the 1965 Immigration Act and the cultural revolution of the 1960s. He also notes that past immigration was European, while 90 percent of new legal immigrants are Asian, African, and Latin American and that they are not "melting and reforming". He continues his marvelous reasoning by suggesting that immigrants generally assimilate more easily into American culture if they come from European cultures and writes, "Any man or any woman, of any color or creed, can be a good American. We know that from our history. But when it comes to the ability to assimilate into a nation like the United States, all nationalities, creeds, and cultures are not equal.et lamented changes in the. "What I would like is — I'd like United States that I grew up in," he said, "It was a good country. I lived in Washington, D.C., - 400,000 black folks, 400,000 white folks, in a country 89 or 90 percent white. I like that country."

It is extremely difficult to hear Pat Buchanan's opinions without first thinking of the palaver of the barnyard animals (Who wants to assimilate into an ass?) I do not wish to be unkind to Pat, but is sounds like his race card has been out in the noon-day sun too long and has become completely bleached white. Presently I am not trying to play the "race card," nor the "green card," but merely present pictures of a multi-colored card-carrier that truly believes in the equality of all humanity. What would Mother Teresa and Gandhi think of our friend Pat? I know; they would have loving thoughts about him. What would Pat do if they immigrated to the U.S.? I know; even though they would not assimilate in dress or always still smell of India, he would learn to love them in spite of his "old" self. He would learn that in the end, it is the heart that should melt and not the pot.

Language Assimilation

As stated before, language usage should not be legislated: one should be able to speak, read, write, and dream in his own tongue; he should not be required to assimilate into the dreams of others. I have no official statistics of how many non-English speakers in this country would seriously like to learn the English language. All I know is that most (if not all) of these non-English speakers that I have met, would love to learn English; they say that their only hindrance is that there are not enough programs here for them to do so. If we do want them to "assimilate," we should then have more programs, no? We could have government-sponsored free Learning-English tapes for all that be viewed on TV, at one's own time, own pace. (FYI, from a linguistic point of view, English is a difficult language to learn, and Spanish is one of the easiest.)

It is difficult for me to believe that I still have to protect my right to speak in Spanish openly. Fifty years ago I was punished for speaking in my "first language" with my friends on the school playground, and today I am still being made ashamed of my Spanish or Spanish accent; in essence considered as a "second class" citizen... pero **No Más!**

This just goes to show that for all the hoopla about "protecting our borders from terrorists," "illegals take our jobs," yakity yak, there appears to be a concerted effort by Anglo America and like supporters to be rid of <u>All Things Latino</u> - their brown bodies, their brown customs, their brown language (but maybe they'll keep their delicious food). Sorry y'all, we ain't going away. Actually we, were here first.

Part VII.

Era of Victimization

Stoneware 36″ H.

Era of Victimization

Victimization – I dislike the word "victimization" for too often many of us hide behind its many syllables – it usually connotes a feeble person that has been hurt/weakened by someone or something and is maimed forever as a consequence, never to rise above their circumstances again. Such a person is then prone to use this "excuse" over and over for not moving forward in their lives. We all feel, in our All-American, rugged, individualism, that when "we're knocked down," we get up by our own "bootstraps" and start (get back on the horse) all over again. Good theory; unfortunately life doesn't fall in place that conveniently. Oh, I have known so many individuals, that as children, have had a parent ridicule them with such language as, "You can't do anything right! You'll never amount to anything! I wish you would have never been born!" Not only have they had to endure such verbal beatings, but have also been physically abused, and in some most horrible cases, sexually violated. It is not an easy task for an individual to recover from such abuses, especially when all three forms have occurred. Oftentimes, there is no healthful recovery. So the word, "victimization" is the perfect word to use in these cases where one person has been truly abused. **Victimization is also no different when entire innocent groups of people or sovereign countries are bullied, stolen from, raped.**

There can also be financial loss and physical injury connected with victimization, but the most devastating part for many victims is the emotional pain caused by the crime. When a victim experiences a stressful event, it is put into a "crisis" mode. A crisis may be caused by an "acute" (one-time) event or "chronic" (repeated) events.

One does not have to stretch their understanding very far to see that the observations of victimized individuals, can definitely be applied to whole countries victimized by the Caucasian Nations in recent history: Most of the countries which we have violated have been left in crisis modes and their peoples left just barely above the gathering of bread crumbs and without much hope. Still stretching this a bit too far? Go dig into history a bit and see if all the massacres and refugees created in Africa in the last half century have not had birth in the tents of white masters. But in spite of past mistakes, I have confidence that with respect, dignity, and compassion on our part, we can help renew the lives of many, especially those seeking aid at our doorsteps.
??? Who said the following? –

> **"You do not wipe away the scars of centuries by saying:**
> **'Now you are free to go wherever you want,**
> **do as you desire, and choose the leaders you please.'**
> **You do not take a man who for years has been hobbled**
> **by chains, liberate him, bring him to the starting line**
> **of a race, saying, 'You are free to compete with all**
> **the others,' and still justly believe you have been completely**
> **fair ... This is the next and more profound stage of civil rights.**
> **We seek not just freedom but opportunity – not just legal**

equality but human ability – not just equality as a right, but equality as a fact and as a result."

Believe it or not, the preceding was expounded by a politician, President Lyndon Johnson, (difficult to believe, maybe it was written by his speech writer), on June 4, 1965. Though of course he was expressing his views on the current issues of civil rights at the time, the statement he made is extremely apropos to what has also happened to Third World countries, and what needs to be done today. In our acts of colonialism, we have left many countries **"shackled,"** and even though we have "freed" them, we still maintain them in an arena of servitude; we still take their resources and basically force them into slave-type conditions of cheap labor exploitations. Sooner or later, we, the "American people," must stop thinking only of ourselves, what's in it for us, what is the best for us. We cannot "drive away the scars of centuries," by merely saying, "Deport them, they are illegal." As President Johnson reasoned wisely, most people not only "seek freedom, but opportunity." **At the starting line of the race of decency, no one has an excuse to cheat others of their humanity.**

Crimes against Americans

No one can disagree that one of the darkest times in American history was the period that allowed for decades of involuntary servitude of a Native African Peoples. Talk about treating people sub-human; the Caucasians took them away from their home place, shackled them, put them to work "black" sweat on their farms, beat them, and sexually abused their women. A hunting dog had more rights and was treated better than these human beings. Besides having finally been given their freedom, were these peoples (race) ever compensated for withstanding, enduring such atrocities of slavery, and later on for "out and out" continued discrimination? Oh, yes. They were first allowed to have their own drinking fountains, their own schools, and their own coveted parts of the bus… the back.

P.O.W.s - Prisoners of Whites?

The United States—with five per cent of the world's population—now houses **25 per cent of the world's prison inmates**. Our incarceration rate—714 per 100,000—is almost 40 per cent greater than those of our nearest competitors (the Bahamas, Belarus, and Russia). More strikingly, it is 6.2 times Canada's rate and 12.3 times that of Japan. In *2007*, I saw on a news TV show, economist Glenn C. Loury, point out that "this extraordinary mass incarceration is not a response to rising crime rates or a proud success of social policy, but that it is the product of a generation-old collective decision to become a more punitive society. Interestingly, and unfortunately, the fact is that changes in our criminal-justice system since the 1970s have created a nether class of Americans—**vastly disproportionately black and brown**—with severely restricted rights and life chances. **A black male resident in the state of California is more likely to go to state prison than to a state college.**" Again how deplorable. How can these situations still exist? We all know the answer: the truth is that even though some people have rid themselves of physical shackles, our white-dominated society still has vast numbers of non-Caucasians bound in history-old habits and traditions. As much as some of us think that we have set the captives free, we still control the lives of others with our subtle racist reigns. Think about this. True or false? The only blacks we have let out of slavery in large numbers are those that have become our athletic heroes, movie stars, those that have achieved rich-and-famous status, and you know, the good-looking ones (with white blood). The latter of course is said facetiously.

Yes, many people now incarcerated have committed crimes and should be punished and "pay their debt to society." But consider this. First, we placed Native Americans in reservations to subjugate them. Next we incarcerated a vast majority of blacks and Latinos and also placed them in reservations, industrial-strength reservations with walls and barbed wire. We made this into quite an industry. We have a corrections sector that employs more Americans than the combined work forces of General Motors, Ford, and Wal-Mart. Remember when we used to punish criminals and tried to rehabilitate them? Well now since we are mainly dealing with non-Caucasians, it appears that we have a collective American justice system that not only wishes to punish its criminals, but also keep them hidden away forever (sort of like out of sight out of mind). Incarceration keeps **them** away from us. If you think that what I am saying is absurd, research this notion for yourself. Again paraphrasing what Glenn C. Loury has stated about Race and the Transformation of Criminal Justice:

"The punitive turn in the nation's social policy— intimately connected with public rhetoric about responsibility, dependency, social hygiene, and the reclamation of public order—can be fully grasped only when viewed against the backdrop of America's often ugly and violent racial history: there is a reason why

our inclination toward forgiveness and the extension of a second chance to those who have violated our behavioral strictures is so stunted, and why our mainstream political discourses are so bereft of self-examination and searching social criticism. This historical resonance between the stigma of race and the stigma of imprisonment serves to keep alive in our public culture the subordinating social meanings that have always been associated with blackness."

"Though we wish to place all of the guilt on the criminal shoulders of "reaping what they have sown," we cannot irresponsibly and immorally deny our "contribution" to this life-long disgrace—for indeed this entire dynamic has its roots in past unjust acts that were perpetrated on the basis of race."

I personally feel we must completely over-haul this three-strike policy.

Has it proven to be a deterrent to crime or merely created more desperation?

"Three Strikes"

Crime, punishment in America has a color—
Cream of darkness, Soul of pain.
Where sand papered, Sun-burnt Skin
Turns to white ash, To be rid of the mark of Cain.
That was a "passer's" plan. Poor and Failed plan.
Now I stand in the middle ghetto, worse than Babylon –
Born to play the streets, the night, "the only game" in town
Since the genes were centuries mutated, scrambled, But privately always afire.
Strike one—blind-folded, swung and missed on a death boat from Afrika.

Led to (Cotton as high as a tobacco Camel's eye.)
Strike two—took the pitch, let the brother steal a bass for the Inner City Blues. Took a deep breath of comfort weed. Calmed the edge of night.
Strike threee—hit the Cop back with his own damn bat. One hit, no home runs, just double trouble.
In a country that loves its game, it's Three strikes, You're out—"for life."
Sent to desert clubs behind walls With towers of mis-guided lights.
No ifs, ands, or buts. No more questions. No more hope in hope.
Never near a breath of reform, forgiveness. Our Lady Justice shows to be more Blind than she thinks.

Seventeen and forever gone—for Life, nightmare bedpans, Eating puke of inner screams—Target of countless Wal-Mart plastic bags as condoms.
"Though must be strong for momma's tears and Thousands of days to make a past complete –
When I visit her grave from the many of mine,
Show what is left in and to my world –
Nothing has changed – Nothing,
I still bleed in cream of darkness
Piss in black."

What do black people have to do with immigration? Nothing and everything. They never did come here on their own volition, but their bodies were definitely abused, raped, and horrifically exploited. Their lives were daily placed in severe crisis; not unlike those of migrants presently here from the South of the Border

and Central America; thus the black and brown motto:
"Work hard, fear hard."

**Discrimination – Why go into the desert of the past
and re-live the scars? Because for some today, the scars
are still raw, scabs are still clinging, not healed, and
unfortunately new ones still continue to be invented
and conceived.** The following are agonizing accounts
perpetuated by Anglo America upon the Mexican and
Mexican-American worker at the early part of the
twentieth century. Some of the people interviewed in a
"truer" sense of history of America had some of these
stories to tell. The stories come from research done by
Ronald Takaki in his comprehensive book, *A Different
Mirror*, 1993. In his text, Professor Takaki presents a
thought-provoking discussion of America as a
multicultural society. A must read for those interested
in a "truer" history of America. Some stories were
different, others were the same ones repeated over and
over again. The following is a collection and disgusting
group of painful words dissected:

- Texas farmers repeatedly offered similar
  explanations for the widespread employment of
  Mexicans: "The white people won't do the work
  and won't live as the Mexicans do on tortillas
  and beans and in one room shacks."
- A deputy sheriff told an interviewer, "Our
  farmers are our best people. They are always
  with us. They keep the country going, but the
  Mexicans are trash. They have no standard of
  living. We herd them like pigs." "If the strike
  continues, it is more than likely that every last
  one of you will be gathered into one huge bull
  pen," a newspaper threatened. "Many of you

don't know how the U.S. government can run a concentration camp....Do you want to face the bull pen? Do you want to be deported to Mexico?

- The wife of an Anglo rancher put it this way: "Let the Mexican have as good an education but still let him know he is not as good as a white man. God did not intend him to be; He would have made them white if He had." For many Anglos, many Mexicans represented a threat to their daughters. "Why don't we let the Mexicans come to the white school?" an Anglo sharecropper angrily declared. "Because a damned greaser is not fit to sit side of a white girl."

- Another Texas superintendent explained why schools should not educate Mexican children: "You have doubtless heard that ignorance is bliss; it seems it is so when one has to transplant onions...If a man has very much sense or education either he is not going to stick to this kind of work. So you see, it is up to the white population to keep the Mexican on his knees in an onion patch.

"I remember in the fifth grade studying Spanish and when we had to do class conversations out loud it was always traumatic for me. Most of the kids in my class were Anglo, so when I spoke Spanish I was careful not to have an accent, so I would not be laughed at. Perhaps I should have shown more will power but it's awfully damned hard when even the teacher snickers. This kind of experience gave me a shyness I have never been able to get rid of. Instead of mastering the language, it was, instead, taken away from me and

replaced by the knowledge that Christopher
Columbus discovered America and that Indians were
savages."

"When we went swimming at the community
swimming pool, the swimming pool was especially
reserved for Mexicans and blacks on Tuesdays and
Wednesdays, not that we were special. The next day
after we had used it, we saw the draining of the "color
stain" from the pool, making the water pure again for
the white Anglo children the remainder of the week."

Because of so many discriminatory acts perpetrated
upon young Mexican-Americans, many developed acute
self-hatred and came to despise their ethnicity and all
that it seemed to signify. **Negative images about
themselves were imprinted on their young souls.** This
hurtful process has continued to today with all the
hullabaloo from Washington politicos for everyone to
assimilate into copies of them. We will not allow our
children to be victimized by cultural imperialism
anymore. **No más.** *Why would anyone want to
assimilate and be like their oppressors, tormentors?
And again as the animales query in the barnyard, "Why
would anyone want to assimilate into an ...?"*

Statue of Liberty - "Brain–drain"

The following poster shows that when it comes to theft
and burglary, the U.S. of A. aims to go "all out." Not
only are we going to exploit your cheap labor, natural
resources, but we shall extract from you the best of your
people (brain-drain). After your country has invested
billions of dollars and years of time educating and
training you, we shall beat the bushes in your

neighborhoods for the best of your best. This is the All-American way. Seek the best; seek to be the best, **número uno**, regardless of what you have to do to reach the top. Besides, you don't want to stay in your "beloved" country, anymore, even though it desperately needs your doctoring hands, your bridge-building skills, your newly acquired magical techniques for finding clean water, and most importantly, a daily embrace for your grandmother. Can one rape a brain?

Studies by the World Bank found that in many developing countries, between 25 and 50% of the college educated population live abroad, while severely under-developed countries like Jamaica and Haiti, the percentage was over 80%. There is a fear that the loss of such a large number of educated people may further fuel the cycle of underdevelopment, given that they not only have needed skills, but also have the ability to be involved in homegrown leadership roles sensitive to their own particular country's needs. Brain drain has cost Africa over $4 billion in the employment of 150,000 expatriate professionals annually. According to the United Nations Development Program, "Ethiopia lost 75% of its skilled workforce between 1980 and 1991," which harms the ability of such nations to get out of poverty. There are more Ethiopian doctors in Chicago than there are in Ethiopia! The UNDP estimates that India loses $2 billion a year because of the emigration of computer experts to the U.S. Forty percent of Ph.D. scientists working in the U.S. were born abroad.

GIVE ME YOUR TECHNICIANS, NURSES, DOCTORS, SCIENTISTS, BUT KEEP YOUR TIRED, HUDDLED MASSES, YOUR POOR.

- ### *S.I.N.*

STOP ICE NOW   STOP ICE NOW   STOP ICE NOW   STOP ICE NOW

Stop the Raids –

I believe that the first act in this discussion on immigration must be the **immediate suspension of the cruel and inhumane raids of I.C.E.** In their blind zeal to uphold the "law," they are kidnapping and terrorizing thousands of individuals daily – in many cases splitting parents from their children, taking husbands away from wives, taking away the only decent livelihood they have known, traumatizing the soul, and creating heartaches upon heartaches.

Americans have **used and abused** people. We have used black slaves, Chinese coolies, and Mexican migrants to build America (I am not saying others didn't also, but these folks were truly exploited the most, while we placed others, buffalo-less on distant reservations). For decades we have "invited" Mexican laborers (and others from around the world) to come and work in our agricultural fields, railroad construction, mines, butchering of all sorts of livestock, cooking and washing dishes in restaurants, making our beds and cleaning our toilets. For doing this, we have paid them sub-standard wages, exploited, cheated, taken advantage of them. Remember the mind pictures in Steinbeck's *The Grapes of Wrath?* If you can imagine, the Mexican migrants had it worse, for they were last on the "totem pole" and even the "Okies" could look down on them.

As proven by the "Chinese Exclusion Act," "Operation Wetback," and now "Operation Return to Sender," we use up people and then at our whim get rid of them; treat them as commodities, like cattle, perhaps more aptly we treat them as an act of husbandry – cultivated oxen, mules. The only problem is that this "stock" has dreams just like their masters. They would also like a part of the life they are helping to create. So, for me to see them being treated as cattle and cockroaches by my fellow Americans is disheartening and unconscionable.

After reading this "study," with all its historical citations on what took place in the theft of Mexican territories, exploitation and abuses of Mexican labor, discrimination of Mexican-Americans, should there be a loud legal call for some forms of **REDRESS, REPARATION**, and **RESTITUTION?** The dictionary seems to say so.

"Redress–n. 1. Reparation, compensation, recompense, payment, indemnification, restitution, rectification, amends, satisfaction, easement, relief. – v. 2. correct, right, set right, rectify, make reparation for, compensate for, make retribution for, amend, make up for, reform, remedy, ease, relieve.

– Syn. Study. 1. REDRESS, REPARATION, RESTITUTION suggest making amends or giving compensation for a wrong. REDRESS may refer either to the act of setting right an unjust situation or to satisfaction sought or gained for a wrong suffered: the redress of grievances. REPARATION refers to compensation or satisfaction for a wrong or loss inflicted. The word may have the moral idea of amends, but more frequently it refers to financial compensation: to make reparation for one's neglect; the reparations demanded of the aggressor nations. RESTITUTION means literally the giving back of what has been taken from the lawful owner, but may refer to restoring the equivalent to what has been taken: The servant convicted of robbery made restitution to his employer."

Center for the Americas

It is understandable that it is extremely difficult, if not impossible, to give back what was has been taken (resources, labor, dignity), but at least we should be open in our minds and hearts to help in some manner those that have been our victims throughout the ages. A possible way to redress our historical miscues is to create specialized centers that would specifically help those in Latin America, African-Americans, and Native Americans in the U.S.

Do not mistake a **Center for the Americas** with **School of the Americas** in Georgia. Before continuing with the proposals for specialized centers, I feel it is imperative to discuss what the U.S. does pro bono, gratis, for free in sponsoring a school for killers.

What is the SOA? The School of the Americas (SOA), in 2001 renamed the "Western Hemisphere Institute for Security Cooperation," is a combat training school for Latin American soldiers located in Benning, Georgia.

Initially established in Panama in 1946, it was kicked out of that country in 1984 under the terms of the Panama Canal Treaty. Former Panamanian President, Jorge Illueca, stated that the School of the Americas was the "biggest base for destabilization in Latin America." The SOA, frequently dubbed the "School of Assassins," has left a trail of blood and suffering in every country where its graduates have returned.

Over its 59 years, the SOA has trained over 60,000 Latin American soldiers in counterinsurgency techniques, sniper training, commando and psychological warfare, military intelligence and interrogation tactics. These graduates have consistently used their skills to wage a war against their own people. Among those targeted by SOA graduates are educators, union organizers, religious workers, student leaders, and others who work for the rights of the poor. Hundreds of thousands of Latin Americans have been tortured, raped, assassinated, "disappeared," massacred, and forced into refugee status by those trained at the School of Assassins.

Proposed Center for the Americas

The Center of the Americas could be an education and research organization established by the U.S. Congress to strengthen relations and understanding among the peoples and nations of the Americas and the United States. The center could contribute to a peaceful, prosperous, and just Latin America community by serving as a vigorous hub for cooperative research, education, and dialogue on critical issues of common concern to Latin American region and the United States. Funding for the Center should come from the U.S. government, with additional support by private agencies, individuals, foundations, corporations, and the governments of the region. As a national and regional resource, the Center could offer: an interdisciplinary research program that examines major issues of critical importance in U.S.-Latin America relations;

Dialogue and professional enrichment programs that focus on groups central to the communication of ideas: the media, political and policy leaders, and educators; educational programs to develop the human resources needed by the United States and the Latin America region in a new era of increased interdependence; and an adjoining hospital or clinic for research and medical services pertinent to needs of Latinos.

Native Peoples Center

A similar national center could be established for Native Peoples (include the BIA in this community) that would focus on the individuality of the many Native tribes that exist in the U.S. Tribes could come together and exhibit their histories – customs, religions, language, and their own particular slant on humanity. Native Hawaiians and Eskimos could find representation here also. Adjacent clinic/hospital would provide health care and a training facility for Native doctors and prospective nurses. Wouldn't such a center provide hope for our young Native-Americans marginalized by centuries of conquerors?

Center for African-Americans

A Center for African-Americans centered on an established first-rate university would enable many black students to obtain a "non-discriminatory" education. Low-income students and those needing an "alternative education" (as in reading readiness, for whatever reasons—be they environmental, intellectual, or maturative—not everyone learns the same or has equal opportunities for learning), could be more properly directed in instruction that would insure better successes to these students. Instruction would be based on "learning" and not on mere grades. They could prove themselves in areas other than athletics, not that they haven't already. Inner-city children need other ways to learn other than having to overcome racist obstacles and poverty. Also a center being connected to African countries would certainly benefit both the African-American students and those that they would be associated with in "sister school" relationships. Specific health care concerns for African-Americans would be addressed here.

And of course we should have a Center for Middle Eastern concerns. Did you know we already have a center in Honolulu for Asian studies, the East-Center?

"The only Humane Thing to do"

It is said that there are about twelve million undocumented immigrants in the U.S.; over half come from Mexico. It is inhumane to deport twelve million individuals after we have in essence invited them to come, work, and live with us for years. It is only humane to give these individuals **amnesty** or start them on some form of **legalization**. The decision should be based on the actions of our hearts plus the "legal" implications of redress for some of the "wrongs" we have caused. It is time to repay some of the debts we owe to these exploited people. But some of you will say, "All of these 'illegals' have burdened our school systems, social programs, prisons, health services, and created millions of dollars of debt owed us." And the Mexican workers will say, "That may be so, but let us 'level the playing cornfield.' You Norteameicanos say you won the Mexican-American War, what we call the "American Invasion" and therefore think you own all of the land you took from us, land from Tejas to California. Yes, you took, but more correctly, you absconded with it as a true history has shown. We suggest you either need to return this land or pay honestly for it plus interest. Plus do you remember all of the times I worked for you and you paid me half of the wages that the white workers received? When I worked your farms and lived in lice-infested chicken coops with my family, and all my children were hurt by alphabet letters like DDT and TB? When we worked twelve-fifteen hours per day, weeding with that hoe from hell?"

Song of "El Cortito" (the little short one)

It always gave of its ripened fruit,
The short hoe from hell,
Long as a devil's foot.
It killed not in seconds
But in countless hours
Of bent-over drops of sweat –
Sweat dripped, released unto dry
dirt clods
Dissolving them for the ages
Into sedimentary soil
For another world to plow

The fruit was often a result in blood,
Not of beets,
But from gnarled, twisted fingers
Carved, sculpted
From quick, sometimes careless hands –
Scarred fleshy tools connected
To mouths of hungry sons and daughters.

(But hands that are quick in the light
Would rather be slow in the dark by desire –
Especially on a woman's shadowed body,
And not slow by reaction
But slow in an instinct of caress.)

Meanwhile dull green leaves of weeds
Toil, pretend to be of value
Cling as frauds, parasites –
In the end prove to be useful
Only to life within themselves.
Is that not reason enough to be?

Not to the patrón.
The weeds are the enemy.
Must be destroyed, pitched
Into an all-consuming fire, eliminated
By men he pays in a few centavos,

Men who sing curses to days of their birth,
That remain stooped
Shaped in the letter n, n, n, n, n
Unable to untangle themselves
For centuries into
Upright human beings.

So you see, you need to pay me the balance of what you
stole from me, plus the interest upon interest. I think
you owe me more than what I owe you. No? I
reasonably understand that you cannot return the land,
but at least let us live in it with you for a long while. Let
us live together in peace as repayment for our lost just
wages and our stolen dignity."

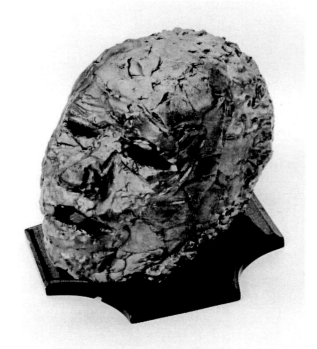

Sonoran Desert Remains - Bronze

"Manifest Destiny"

I am a wandering seed,
Planted by the truest Version and Vision
Of Manifest Destiny.

Go ahead
Take my picture

I will not appear
For I have disappeared
Into a muted darkness
That only thieves, fears create.
I have become
The shadow of a lost name.

My barbed-wire scars are still raw.

Invisible, I have become your toilet scrubber.
In silence, I have become your dust blower.
In limbo, I have become the maid that
Floats, hides behind a mirage of scorching heat –
As I wait, thirst, for a city bus.

Secret and exotic recipes I have shared with your
dull tastes,
Even suckled your children at my teat.
So tell me in and with your eyes, do you know
that I live the way I do,
So you can live the many ways you wish to?

But yet, like the unfailing Primavera
That returns, remembers, dreams –
I too am pregnant
With buds, desert rain, fruit of the Earth,
Fragrant HOPE.

But still, the thunder in my heart wonders,

"Since I am an eternal soul,
Why must I beg for work,
Like a leper, sneak back into my own house?"

Sound the Alarm?

I do not want to be an "alarmist," but I feel in this day and age, we must begin making friends, instead of more enemies. Knowingly or unknowingly we are making many enemies now for the future of our children. For decades, no one has ever come from south of the border to bring us terror, unlike the Timothy McVey we grew from within, and those that came from beyond the sea. The U.S. is in a momentous crossroads situation; we can either use our riches and power to help others, or merely use our strengths to be greedier, consume more, create more injustices around the world – and thus make more enemies. We do not want to turn friendly neighbors who are only desirous of bread for their families into bearers of **flaming flames of terrorism.** No bombs, rockets, bullets are required; just xxxxxxcensoredxxxx can start Nero's whole world burning again. No creature fighting for its life, whether black, white, or brown likes to be cornered. Sooner or later, **it will fight back**. When are we going to learn to make friends? Do we truly think an 800 mile fence is going to protect us from "friends" which we are daily making our enemies. Not even the distance of a 4,000 mile ocean kept us safe once. Remember? All that most people want, just above a loaf of bread, is to be treated with dignity.

And conscionably, in order to bring a deserved justice to our past, America must truthfully put flesh and clothing on the skeletons that we have had hidden in our silent history closets for centuries: the yellow skeleton of the Gold Rush in 1849, Chinaman that got cheeky, was hung for looking at the beauty of a white woman; the black one drowned after being weighted down with an industrial fan and thrown into an Alabama river for avenging the raping of his wife; the red one stripped of skin and hung from the tallest pole in his teepee, guilty for being in America first; and the brown one dangling outside of San Antonio from a cottonwood with a sign around his collar, and which still reads in fresh blood, fresh pain: **No Dogs – No Mexicans**.

Though this report dealt more or less with local physical immigration, there is a greater form of emigration taking place in this world, which we must never forget – that which has people grasping tenderly and untiringly for their own version and vision of **"Manifest Destiny."** All around the world, their dreams shall finally move/cross them through the "Guardians of the Flyway," those ugly fences and borders of caste, abuses of women, prejudices of color/race, poverty, senseless wars… and our unjust hearts. **No one deserves to live stuck in a silent scream.**

War upon War

As stated before, war plays a major part in creating homeless, destitute refugees, which in their plight to merely survive eventually end up becoming immigrants to a "host" country be it legally or illegally. Of course the war/fire starters never think of this; they truly don't "bleed" thoughts that many innocent people will be innocent no more once the bombs and bullets fall. And more importantly blood falls. Everyone agrees that history should teach us lessons against gross stupidity, but it seems that every 25-30 years, we start all over. We must be entertained by a new folly. Either our sagging memories let us down or we truly have a misguided need to show our young the most highly uncreative game to play – the game of death. Believe it or not I write this part in this report so that someone around in the year 2030 will take heed -- don't be fooled by politicians' fear of fear, and please for the sake of all that flowers, do not be SILENT.

"We're No. 1!" "We're No. 1." In World Arms Sales

Yearly, U.S. arms sales to the Third World run in the tens of billions of dollars making it the number one supplier of killing implements worldwide. And we who get upset at those who would dare point out our hypocrisy when we claim to be champions of human rights and peace around the world. Yes, chant it loudly, We're number one!"

And believe it or not, we place Holy Bible scriptures on the rifles used for killing in Iraq and Afghanistan. God help us.

SILENCE IS CONSENT (Year 2004)
Road to War
I.

In the History of Hell
Age of War, PRIDE that blinds,
creates Mass acres of Massacres;
Corpses dance upon each other,
Have sex with many partners,
Unknowingly, Seemingly
With their own children.

While Helmeted vultures disguised as crows
Scavenge, pick, Mine
for golden treasures In teeth of gaping mouths,
that call out for Help, a Final rest –
"*Bury me*," they cry, "*before the Sun rises,
the Gothic forest gasps a deathly stench.*"

Sadly a saving Breath of Life dangling from
silken skies
Arrived months too late (As Chagall fiddlers fell
off grassy roofs)
And Angel Makers glowed. Didn't you know?
Really?
Red-hot Kilns, did not merely bake kosher
bread?
They toasted more than sausage flesh –
The gingerbread man, his child, his bride?
As graveyard secrets
A fence of the ages more than kept –
"SILENCE was not Golden,
but of deepest Black,
And Ash fell nightly –

Crisp and charred
As fleshly Snow."

II.

Jungle gym. Jungle warfare.
Worlds apart, children of one at play –
Flaming Children of Rice in another gather
Tattered, Charcoal-dusted arms, legs –
No longer able to stroke a violin,
Chase a kite, Flee a cloud of Orange,
Write a bamboo poem.

As inscripted sacred words demand that '**Life is
in the Blood,**'
Lionesque Fountains filled
With a warrior's sanguinary liquid,
    'surely more precious than gold,'
Spout high as geysers;
Overflow into lifeless seas of Repeated history –
Battle years and Fears of **imaginary Falling
Dominos**.

III.

Soon Heroes Come Marching Home,
But Wait…*Take a quick smell of a flower*
           **For soon peace will be but for an
hour.**
A familiar Story comes high-stepping
'Round the corner in an all-knowing smirk
As Presidents re-make memories of Purple
Hearts, MIAs, POWs,
Hide the History Books between
    Mother Goose---AND---Aesop's Fables,

While Solomon's Wisdom cries out in the Streets,
"There Is Nothing New Under The Sun!" Or should
it be,
**"There is no new news, just Old News happening
to new people."**

[America listens to itself in Quiet Silence.]

Thus Little Boy Blue is encouraged
To lead other young boys to Siphon
their blood again into 55-gallon Oil Drums
with the Blow of his patriotic horn.
And once again Little Lost Sheep will fall asleep
Into dusty, sandy meadows deep
And Blind Mice will die to an anger Foreign
born.

"Less graves, More gardens," pleads the sobbing
Earth
As it no longer yearns
To be a bed for young seeds scattered in vain.

But still Americans are asked to support more
Wars
The Chess players cannot check, nor win.
We Must remain still, in dullness;
    Prove to all we are asleep –
In a mirage where "Might Makes Right,"
            Silence is Consent.

The preceding poem was written in 2004, where and when no collective voices of protest could be seen or heard, and indeed "Our Silence" was "Our Consent." I am truly thankful that most Americans are now wiping away the sleep from their eyes and are beginning to see beyond the words that the politicos weave to dull us into their private dreams – when in reality their imaginings are nightmares in disguise, decorated coffins for the oldest of our young.

What's it all about? Life or death? Or is it usually about the mere **military scare tactics of giant falling dominos** that those in the Government hierarchy use to promote their private ideologies and hence their wars…"If Vietnam falls, SE Asia will fall, Taiwan will fall, and next the commies will be knocking down the Hollywood sign." Today we trade in the millions of dollars with Vietnam, and the last time I looked through the LA smog, the Hollywood sign was still there. So what was "that" all about? The same thing occurred in Central America. "If El Salvador falls, Honduras will fall, Guatemala will fall, and the war will cross across the Rio Grande to Brownsville (Texas)." The only thing that fell was the price of bananas from Guatemala you all get today at Wal-Mart. Nothing of true importance fell – nothing again except large drips of innocent blood on both sides fell on the hallowed ground of a future, ignored history. Through these wars, how many innocent souls were made homeless, physically and politically and made refugees and immigrants.

When we make a mistake, we must "own up to it," and move on. But, Americans hate to lose at anything, and as in Vietnam, today's Politicians and Military Generals keep sending in more to troops to prove to others that their campaigns were/are not failures. In camouflaged rhetoric (in reality protecting their own behinds by playing on our vulnerable heartstrings), they vehemently assert, "If we 'give-up' now, those soldiers that died, would have died in vain." The truth is that as much as we hate to hear it, believe it, some "innocent" U.S. soldiers have died; and continue to die, at the hands of powerful political and military lips that are full of commands and orders that wish to continue upon their proven-failed policies. And unfortunately as in Vietnam, their selfish, simple-minded, protect-oneself, save-thy-face notions come at the tremendous cost of young blood doing its "duty." Enough is enough. No más. We must put an end to the sanguine flow. And thus, we will ultimately find true Honor.

By the way, have you ever read Dr. King's paper on the Vietnam War? If you haven't, you should. Some think it is just as incisive and riveting as his "I have a Dream" Speech.

In parting –

"My Dearest Child, know that ye does not seek to satisfy a death for me, nor for Thy country, but for the King. Know that ye are neither my Protector, my Deliverer, nor my Savior. I pray ye soon become wise, awaken from Thy sacred slumber and teach Thyself to live in Peace with all men.

And Dear One, I say this in deepest sincerity, even though I hate war, abhor killing, that if Freedom was truly threatened in America by the conflicts in Iraq, Afghanistan, Vietnam, El Salvador, etc. and not by mere Washingtonian hubris, Political Pride, I would be the first to "sign up" to defend, fight, and die for my country, my children, ...and for you."

"Collateral Damage"- Aluminum 40"H.

Soldier talk on PBS. "Is this a Vietnamese 'gook' or an Arab 'hadji?' No matter. They are all sub-human anyway. Collateral damage makes them all the same."

Question: Is it also "collateral damage" when U. S. citizens/ranchers might be "accidently" killed by night travelers on the way to their "Promise Land?"

Part VIII.

Addendum- Solutions?
New Issues 2010

"Mayan Princess"-36"High

"Mountain that Eats Men"

Before we get started on the solutions portion in this Part, I'd like to show you something that I recently ran across on a television news clip about a **"mountain that eats men."** This mountain with an avarice appetite is located near the highest city in the world, Potosí, Bolivia, 14,000 feet above sea level. The program went on to say that mining has defined Potosí for almost five centuries, but it has always come with a heavy price. In the 1500s, one of the local Indians leaked the secret of the vast veins of silver in "el Cerro Rico," the "rich mountain" that towers over Potosí, and the Spanish then started up a system of forced Indian labor to dig out the treasure. <u>Between 1545 and 1824, about **8 million** "Indians" and African slaves died in the process of producing between 22,000 and 45,000 tons of silver for the Spanish Empire.</u> Not to belabor the point, but again the rape of an innocent victim has occurred and the bloody illegitimate child (precious stolen metal) has been taken away to be the "seed" to finance Caucasian empires. It said that so much silver was "extracted" from this one mine, that it provided enough wealth to finance the entire Spanish conquest of the Americas. Others have also stated that the riches taken to Europe from such mines in the Americas, aided greatly in stimulating the bringing forth of the European Industrial Revolution.

Today, the mountain is no longer called "el Cerro Rico," though unfortunately it still claims its title of "the mountain that eats men," and it still continues to cry about the fact that the city it once made the richest in the world, richer than Paris or London, has become one of the poorest in the Americas. Mining still occurs in "el

Cerro Rico," but mostly what is extracted now is iron, zinc, tin, and lead by native descendents and their children. Many of the children chew on coca leaves to "give them strength" to endure the hardships they face hidden in the dark – long hours, limited air, toxic materials, and little food. And of course they must always be alert for the biting jaws of the "mountain that eats men," for many of its tunnel vessels are in ill-repair and occasionally constrict, crumble upon young teen-age sacrifices. Do you think that any of these survivors have any idea that their artisan ancestors once created breathless golden treasures alongside exquisite pottery and weavings? They have no idea because they have never seen nor touched these "national treasures" for they were once "kidnapped" and are now hiding openly in museums of the West. Will the young of the Third World ever have the opportunity to feel proud of the great artifacts that their ancestors created?

So, what has this all have to do with solutions? When I heard the story of the "mountain that eats men," again I thought that we, the nations benefitting from these unjust thefts, have a great responsibility to rectify detrimental situations we have caused around the world. I believe that we all must have a vision for this and since this is a global problem, it requires global involvement and global solutions. Do I believe that "we are our brothers' keepers?" Of course, especially since we were the ones that created tremendous problems for the "brother."

Solutions?

First let's look at some of the solutions often presented on the Internet:

1.   Punish the business owners who hire "illegals."

2. Legalize the illegals currently here who haven't committed additional crimes beyond those needed to earn a respectable living.

3. Ship all 12,000,000 back. No amnesty. Not even a whisper of "forgiveness."

4. Build a wall greater than the Great Wall of China.

5. Come out of shadows. Pay a fine and get back at the end of an endless line. (Sure! A line that does not exist.)

6. Kill off the guest worker program for all but critical industries (agri- business) and force employers to offer wages above the prevailing wage before they can ask for immigrant labor.

7. Make it harder to overstay a visa or cross into the USA illegally.

8. E-verify. Make it impossible to hire any person without a secure ID issued by the state and without passing the federal employment database.

9. Anchor your boat, baby, but not in the U.S. of A.

10. Make all surrender their privilege of speaking in tongues. English only.

For those who like to take the "high moral ground" of "we are a nation of laws and the illegals are making a mockery of them." **Did you know that President Ronald Reagan broke three million of these laws in 1986. "I believe in the idea of amnesty for those who have put down roots and lived here, even though some time back they may have entered illegally," as he declared justice with his pen.**

Legalization /Amnesty

Legalization or Amnesty?

What's the difference between **comprehensive immigration reform**, **legalization**, and **amnesty**? The following are points which AFSC (American Friends) repeatedly stress in presenting their view on Immigration.

1. *Comprehensive immigration reform, legalization, amnesty, earned adjustment, regularization, normalization* — all of these terms refer in some way to providing legal status to undocumented immigrants. They differ in their approach to how immigrants should obtain legal status or for how long this legal status should last. Depending on who is using the terms, they can refer to extremely different concepts.

2. Most people — immigrants, advocates, and policy makers — refer to the measures adopted in 1986 as an **"amnesty."** The Immigration Reform and Control Act of 1986 (IRCA) allowed undocumented immigrants who had been living in the United States since before January 1, 1982, to apply for permanent residency.

3. Immigrant activists and other immigrants' rights advocates believe it is detrimental and unjust for a society to create an underclass of individuals with fewer rights or without the ability to exercise their human rights. Therefore, they believe that undocumented immigrants should be granted full legal status. Under current U.S. law, that is "lawful permanent resident" (LPR) status, which can later lead to the opportunity to apply for citizenship. According to the most basic definition above, what immigrants and advocates are pushing for is an amnesty.

4. In the years since the passage of IRCA, the word "amnesty" has become a political hot potato —

tossed around by proponents and opponents of the concept in order to label the other side. Immigrants and advocates who support amnesty are of two minds about the term "amnesty." Some say that "amnesty" means extending LPR status to undocumented immigrants; this is what happened in 1986, and it is what needs to happen again whether or not it includes other measures. In addition, it is a term that immigrant communities understand, especially the Spanish-speaking community with the translation "amnestía."

5. Within the immigrants' rights community, others argue that, although they also support granting LPR status to undocumented immigrants, legislators in Congress are unwilling to even begin a conversation if the term "amnesty" is used. Therefore, they prefer the term "legalization." Some would also say that there is a substantive difference between the concepts of "legalization" and "amnesty," in that "legalization" would include a more stringent application process or other provisions, including measures to regulate future flows of migration. At the same time, however, others would argue that the concepts are exactly the same; the difference is simply the term.

Proponents of the term "legalization" argue that "amnesty" implies "forgiveness" for a "crime." Immigration, they believe, should not be seen as a crime. Proponents of the term "amnesty" say that no human being is illegal, and so they do not need to ask for "legalization." "Amnesty," they believe, is the more appropriate term, because it asks forgiveness for breaking a law, albeit an unjust law. Amnesty International, for example, has been using the term for years, but it does not cast political prisoners in a negative light. And so, the debate continues.

6. Those who oppose providing legal status to undocumented immigrants have vilified the word "amnesty" so much that President Bush, in his January 7th statement on immigration reform, declared, "I oppose amnesty, placing undocumented workers on the automatic path to citizenship." It is important to note that President Bush implied yet another definition of "amnesty," which differs from those we have offered so far.

7. Members of Congress from both parties refrain from using the word "amnesty." Some use "legalization." Other terms are also used occasionally, including, "earned adjustment," "regularization," and "normalization." Earned adjustment tends to imply that the applicants for legal permanent resident status must "earn" their right to LPR status by promising to work additional years or fulfilling some other requirement besides having been an important member of the community for years. As a result, they may be granted some kind of "conditional" status before receiving LPR status. At times, regularization and normalization refer to granting temporary legal status, for example through a guest worker program, rather than permanent residency. There have also been occasions, however, when these two terms have

been used by policy makers as synonyms of legalization.

AFSC advocates for the full recognition and protection of the human rights of all people, including immigrants to the United States, documented or undocumented. Regardless of which term is used, AFSC affirms that, under U.S. laws and on a policy level, protecting the human rights of all requires, at the very least, providing LPR status to undocumented immigrants.

"Queueless on Immigration"

(Or, a non-professional or a poor person doesn't stand a "Chinaman's" chance of getting back in.)

Quotes By Shikha Dalmia in 2007
Shikha Dalmia has adroitly stated,

- "For two decades, immigration bashers have stymied any attempt to regularize the status of illegal aliens in this country by employing one, single trope against them: they are queue-jumpers who illegally crossed the border ahead of those patiently waiting their turn."

- "But the trope is a fallacy based on a complete mis-statement of U.S. immigration policy. There is no such line - a legal pathway to citizenship for unskilled workers. Still, this unfair accusation has transformed 'amnesty' into a dirty word. Equally bad, it has made a guest worker program for future unskilled workers contingent on first creating a Berlin Wall on the Mexican border."

- "This last rationale is what the queue-jumping trope powerfully undercuts by suggesting that amnesty for illegals means depriving someone else, more worthy, of entry into the country. Worse, it implies that undocumented workers actually have a choice of taking the legal road just like those waiting in line, but choose to willfully ignore it."

- **"In essence, there is no queue for unskilled workers to stand in. Amnesty for them therefore has zero bearing on the wait time of skilled workers. And without amnesty, there is no way currently for them to become permanent residents - much less citizens. Creating such a way for future unskilled workers through a guest-worker program ought to be the top goal of any sensible immigration reformer."**

- **"The so-called problem of illegal immigration is purely the creation of America's restrictive immigration laws. But the queue-jumping trope has allowed immigration opponents to seize the moral high-ground and make the enforcement of these restrictive policies the issue, rather than their reform."**

Visa Overstay

A tourist or traveler is considered a "visa overstay" once he or she remains in the United States after the time of admission has expired. The time of admission varies greatly from traveler to traveler depending on what visa class into which they were admitted. Visa overstayers tend to be somewhat more educated and better off financially than those who entered the country illegally in other ways. To get a tourist visa, a person has to show they have substantial ties to their home country - in the form of a job, school, or family. And most of these people already have enough money to fly into the country. "As a class, they're educated, skilled, and innovative. They're willing to take jobs Americans won't," says Allan Wernick, chairman of the Citizenship and Immigration Project at the City University of New York. "They're a tremendous boost to the economy."

Visa overstayers mostly enter with tourist or business visas. In 1994, more than half of "illegal immigrants" were Visa overstayers whereas in 2006, about 45% of illegal immigrants were Visa overstayers.

Question: If nearly one-half of "illegal immigrants" to the US were Visa overstayers, how does that warrant such a tremendous focus on a mere wall?

"Anchor Babies"

The term "anchor baby" or 'drop baby" assumes that having a US citizen child confers immigration benefits on the parents and extended family. This is generally a false assumption, as immigration law does not allow a US citizen child to sponsor his parents until **he or she turns 21.** Once the child turns 18, immigration law also allows a US citizen child to sponsor his own siblings with a 15 to 23 year quota delay. Immigration law does not provide categories for any other relatives that would apply in this situation. In addition, if the parents are illegal immigrants, they are usually barred from immigration despite having a sponsor.

In the public debate surrounding "anchor babies", it is also frequently assumed that an "anchor baby" would be beneficial in deportation proceedings. Such benefits do not exist except in the very rare case of extreme and profound hardship on the child. Approximately 88,000 legal immigrant parents of US citizen children have been deported in the past ten years for what it described as "minor criminal convictions" now classified as aggravated felonies, including nonviolent drug offenses, simple assaults and drunk driving. Federal appellate courts and the Supreme Court have upheld the refusal by ICE to stay the deportation of illegal immigrants merely on the grounds that they have U.S.-citizen, minor children.

So it seems that those that whine about boat loads of "anchor babies" being dropped on our desert shores have some messy diapers of their own to take care of.

E-Verify

E-Verify is an Internet based, free program run by the United States Government that compares information from an employee's Employment Eligibility Verification Form I-9y to data from U.S. government records. If the information matches, that employee is eligible to work in the United States. If there's a mismatch, E-Verify alerts the employer and the employee is allowed to work while he or she resolves the problem within eight days. The program is operated by the Department of Homeland Security (DHS) in partnership with the Social Security Administration.

According to the DHS website, more than 196,000 employers now use E-Verify. Over 1,400 companies enroll in the program every week. The program was originally established in 1997 as the **Basic Pilot Program** along with two other programs created to prevent undocumented aliens from getting jobs.

All employers, by law, must complete Form I-9. E-Verify is closely linked to Form I-9, but participation in **E-Verify is voluntary for most employers.** After an employee is hired to work for pay, the employee and employer complete Form I-9. After an employee begins work for pay, the employer enters the information from Form I-9 into E-Verify. E-Verify then compares that information against millions of government records and returns a result.

About 5 percent of queries are identified as "not authorized to work". A 2008 Center for Information Studies. Backgrounder states that the E-Verify system is 99.5 percent accurate.

There are several state laws regarding the requirement and prohibition of E-Verify for employers. The state of Arizona requires employers to participate in E-Verify: the *Legal Arizona Workers Act* has survived a number of constitutional challenges and is currently in effect. The Legal Arizona Workers Act requires all Arizona employers to use E-verify with all newly hired employees, effective January 1, 2008. As of December 2008, 5.6 percent of Arizona businesses had signed up with E-verify. Republicans who hate federal government intervention in business love this law. Pick and choose?

More than 212,000 employers are enrolled in the program, with over 8.7 million queries run through the system in fiscal year 2009. There have been over 12 million queries run through the system in fiscal year 2010 (as of July 10, 2010).

E-Verify is mandatory for some employers, such as those employers with federal contracts or subcontracts that contain the Federal Acquisition Regulation (FAR) E-Verify clause and employers in certain states.

"The Dream Act"

The **Development, Relief and Education for Alien Minors Act** (The "DREAM Act") is a piece of proposed federal legislation in the United States that was introduced in the United States Senate, and the United House of Representatives on March 26, 2009. This bill would provide certain undocumented immigrant students who graduate from US high schools, who are of good moral character, arrived in the U.S. as minors, and have been in the country continuously for at least five years prior to the bill's enactment, the opportunity to earn conditional permanent residency. The alien students would obtain temporary residency for a six year period. Within the six year period, a qualified student must have "acquired a degree from an institution of higher education in the United States or have completed at least 2 years, in good standing, in a program for a bachelor's degree or higher degree in the United States," or have "served in the uniformed services for at least 2 years and, if discharged, have received an honorable discharge." Any alien whose permanent resident status is terminated according to the terms of the Act shall return to the immigration status the alien had immediately prior to receiving conditional permanent resident status under this Act. Alien minors in the United States can only obtain permanent status through their parents; there is no independent method to accomplish this. If a child is brought into the country without immigration visas there is no method for becoming a documented resident. Returning to their country of birth would not guarantee a path to documented status. Attempts to return are often difficult, with roadblocks such as ten year bans on re-entering the U.S.

Members of Congress have introduced several forms of this bill in both the House of Representatives and the Senate. Members in the House have not brought the bill to a floor vote as a stand-alone bill; Senators debated a version of the DREAM Act S.2205 on October 24, 2007. The bill, which required 60 votes to gain cloture, failed on a 52-44 vote, 8 votes short of overcoming a filibuster by senators opposed to the bill.

The United States military faced challenges in enlistment, which in 2005 were described as a "crisis" by some. Immigrants who do not have a "green card" are not technically allowed to enlist (although unlawful exceptions are sometimes made due to enlistment shortfalls). Several senior officials at the Department of Defense have spoken in favor of promising legal status to members of the military as a means of boosting recruitment. **"You can't Live with us, but you can Die with us."** Remember this from the repeal of the Chinese Exclusion Act during WWII?

In the previous sections of this report it was mentioned that we should entertain the idea that possible REDRESS, REPARATIONS, and RESTITUTION were in order in varying degrees to correct our discriminate and unjust actions upon other sovereign peoples. Perhaps another "R" which is just as important should be added in this dilemma: REDEMPTION. The Western Nations, instead of punishing people for coming into their country illegally in search of work, now have a great opportunity to rectify past "indiscretions," by truly focusing on the problems the future immigrants face daily in their home countries. A vast majority would not leave if they had even the simplest means of survival – like clean water, ample food, medical facilities, a small plot of land, chickens, a goat or two – the "All-Third-World Dream." Imagine: One day waking up at 4:30 in the morning. Make yourself two bean and chile burritos for the road. Kiss your three young children on the forehead without waking them. Kiss your sick wife on the cheek as you say a soft "good-bye." And as a final task before you embark on your three thousand mile journey (on foot) to the North, you stop at the neighborhood church where you say a quick prayer to the poly-chrome, wooden Virgen. The flickering candles create the illusion that the Virgen is opening and closing her eyes, and that she is talking to you. You ask for a safe trip, and that she takes care of your loved ones while you are gone. You are not certain when you will see them again, if ever again. Outside, you take a deep breath of the coolness and of the individual smells in the courtyard of your youth. Is this truly a final good-bye? You think to yourself, "Why am I leaving all that I love – mi familia, mi casa, mi pueblo, mi querido país (my dear country)?" You know the answer, for it has come to you hundreds of times before: "I must go. I must feed my family. There is no work here. The rich have taken all the good land. They work with foreign gringos, and they gather all the riches of our country for themselves. I must find food for my family."

Unfortunately the above story is sadly multiplied thousands of times, if not millions, all over world – they do not want to leave but are forced to do so. So what is the solution to this problem? Well, perhaps we can kill two pájaros with one stone. How about this idea? It is known that most Americans cringe upon hearing the word **"amnesty."** They feel that providing amnesty without any consequences (punishment, shipped out, fined) makes a "travesty" of our code of laws, now and for the future. What if we charged, not fined, each undocumented immigrant one thousand (arbitrary figure) dollars for staying in this country and becoming a naturalized citizen, provided they had been in this country at least two years (also arbitrary figure), and had not committed any felonies. Any child born in the U.S. would be exempt from paying the charge. The charge could be paid in (within) three years, with APR interest charged on the balance.

Now the preceding recommendation would take care of those circa twelve million undocumented immigrants living in the U.S. today. What about the continual flood of those wishing to come to the U.S. legally or forced to come illegally? This is where the other half of the stone becomes a major part in curtailing the main reason people come here illegally, and that would be for extreme poverty. Recall the monies charged to those wanting to stay in the U.S.? Those billions of dollars would be used to improve the economical conditions of the places, regions from where the major "illegals traffic" would be coming from, be it Mexico, Honduras, Guatemala, etc. The U.S. and the countries emitting immigrants would work together in setting up industries, agricultural ventures, taking care of health and sanitation needs, literacy programs, and create other opportunities through such highly successful ventures provided through a "recent" innovation, "micro-credit."

Microcredit- Since not everyone may be acquainted with this concept, let me say a few words on this. Microcredit is the extension of very small loans (microloans- from $100 to $300) to the unemployed, to poor entrepreneurs, and to others living in poverty who are not considered *bankable*. These individuals lack collateral, steady employment and a verifiable credit history and therefore cannot meet even the most minimal qualifications to gain access to traditional credit. But with a small loan for example, some can start an entire sewing industry with the purchase of a sewing machine, some can sell milk, make cheese with the acquisition of a fine goat, while others only need a few items to mend and polish shoes. **There has been truly no lack of entrepreneurial ideas, only lack of available funds.**

  Microcredit as a financial innovation originated in faraway Bangladesh, where it successfully enabled extremely impoverished people to engage in self-employment projects that allow them to generate an income and many cases begin to build wealth and exit poverty. Due to the success of microcredit, many in the traditional banking industry have begun to realize that these microcredit borrowers should more correctly be categorized as *pre-bankable*; thus, microcredit is increasingly gaining credibility in the mainstream finance industry and many traditional large finance organizations are contemplating microcredit projects as a source of future growth. Most of the loans were granted to women (unfortunately men were more likely to squander the borrowed money on booze and gambling) for they are more responsible in taking care of the family's food needs and for the education of their children. (For more information read "Mohammad Yunus, Banker to the Poor." Great book.

Industry- "Hecho en Mexico." (Made in Mexico.)

Years ago it was quite common to see this label on many goods sold in the U.S. Now of course, millions of labels say, "Made in China." Ideally for us, "Made in U.S.A." labels would be in our best interest, but no "All-Americans" will work for such incredible low wages as the foreigners do. Throughout my years in the small business world, I've owned several gift shops. And of course most of the goods I sold were "made in China." What was quite amazing to me was: 1.) The goods from China were very inexpensive. 2.) The goods were of high quality for the price. 3.) The packaging was well-designed in order to avoid breakage. 4.) And lastly, the giftware was readily available. It could be easily ordered and restocked in about ten days. So all of this got me wondering, "Why can't similar China models be done here closer to home, like in Mexico?" Mexico does appear to have large of amounts of surplus labor. Also a great advantage of this would of course be savings in shipping costs. I must admit I do not know all of the ramifications of being involved in such economic ventures to the south of our borders. Again though, the focus is to provide jobs in particular areas so that people do not have to migrate illegally to the U.S. And again, the initial funds to aid in the development of foreign industries would come from monies collected from immigrant workers wishing to receive "amnesty" and reside permanently in the U.S. Government grants and private investment could also be used to supplement the "financial pool" needed to begin and continue such an ambitious endeavor.

The Program- **"The Peace Action Solutions Organization"** (**PASO** means step or passage). How would it work? Of course the host countries would have to be in agreement in partnering in such a program. But who would not appreciate being "paid back" with, or at least in the value of, something that had been "borrowed" (land, golden metals, slave labor) years before? And wouldn't this PASO (step) be of great benefit to the country's poor? But like the "Prime Directive" in *Star Trek,* it should be clearly understood that there can be no interference with the internal affairs of the host countries; they must be afforded the freedom of complete self-determination, for after all, this is what they were dearly forced to surrender years before.

So who should be recruited to start up such an undertaking? Possibly ex-Peace Corps Volunteers working with experienced business people? I am certain that most Returning Volunteers, as they are known, still have a great remnant of idealism which initially called them – they feel that they can make a difference in this world by helping others. And by now there are thousands of these highly motivated returnees willing to take on new challenges. These people would be willing to endure hardships, would already know the host language, and above all have a great sense of cultural sensitivity, which without it, most foreigners get themselves in muchas problemas or turn themselves quickly into the **Ugly American**. And to them, it would not be "about the money."

Details as to how to begin, oversee, and make such a needed "payback" program successful, will have to be saved for another day and for those that are more experienced that I am in the world of agri-business, health care, education, industry, economics, and finance. What I do know after studying this highly emotional topic of immigration for over two years, is that it is a **global problem, not just a disagreeable situation on the U.S.-Mexican border. And that it was initially created by the colonial powers of the West, and furthermore that today it is acerbated daily by the continual exploitation of the world's poor in an era of globalization – there is still the stealing of land, the raping of resources, and unfortunately the use of near slave-like labor.**

Yes, "America, the Beautiful," is beautiful and bountiful. To me, all countries are "beautiful." They all have their own inherent beauty in the land, whether they be steaming-hot, mirage-filled deserts, be full of sunset canyons, or taste and smell of lush rain forests. The sad thing is that most countries around the world are not bountiful- some would say that this is so because the inhabitants there are "just born lazy." History would vehemently disagree. It would tell of a true story of countless "peoples of color" around the world subjugated for the last five hundred years by Caucasian colonials. Not true? Where are the Australian aborigines in an entire continent that was their own that became a dumping ground for English criminals? Talking about criminals, how many years did Nelson Mandela spend in South African prisons to rid of the scourge of apartheid?: DURBAN (1989) – **THIS BATHING AREA IS FOR SOLE USE OF THE WHITE GROUP**. This sign in the Dark Continent?

Where are the Native Americans? In reservation restaurants without buffalo burgers on the menu? Listening on the native drums that the Great White Fathers in Washington want only English spoken in the hogans and teepees, because this is after all the America of Tom Tancredo and Pat Buchanan? Where are the black people once taken from their African villages? Now in villages of inner-city housing projects where even Dr. David Livingstone would not presume and dare to enter? Where are all the Spanish-speaking peoples of the Southwest who have not "assimilated" in an area that once was theirs (Mexican)? Someone once asked in a song, "Where have all the flowers gone, long time passing?" I think some of us know. The flowers are still in the shadows calling out, **"Why do we have to live stuck in a silent scream?"**

Every year in the U.S., we have countless holidays to celebrate on the most part historical events. Unfortunately these "holy days" have proven to be mere super- colossal commercial bombardments by and for the benefit of Madison Avenue. Do we **really need** little plastic eggs, a witch's costume, Christmas lights so that the Jolly Fellow's reindeer can find the chimney we don't have? And then, there is the most obligatory act, we must wave that tiny American flag (made in China) to prove to all that we are patriotic through and through, even though flags are symbols that mostly unite people, against others. And then there's the eating and drinking. (I like this part too.) Some of us feed our fat faces till we pass out; even though we are not pregnant, we grind as if were eating for two or three. Sometimes many of us fall into a stupor wondering if someone has spiked our booze with powders of tryptophan.

Day(s) of Atonement- Perhaps to counter balance these meaningless attempts to take time out from the weekly, mundane routines we could have a time of serious reflection, whether it be on a personal or national level. Every year there should be a time whereby we deeply examine our relationships with others; be they our God, our relatives, neighbors, co-workers, others. Most of us I dare say have better "relationships" with our TV characters than with our neighbors. Some of us probably don't even know our neighbors' names. Guilty here. The main concern in this holy day is that we <u>repair a damaged relationship</u>, possibly by even fasting as we deeply reflect on an offense we may have with someone. Then comes the tricky part. Can we possibly muster enough humbleness and strength to ask for forgiveness, and then make some reparation, compensation, or amends if such are required? An impossible task, especially at the national level? Some of us can dream. And how about this for a radical idea of atonement: in order to aid struggling countries into stable economic futures, perhaps every citizen of the West could contribute 5% of his wages for three years as seed money to create a balance of economic growth. I would be more than willing to make this sacrifice, since such sacrifices have been going on for hundreds of years for me.

Finally, in an introduction of another emphatic "R" word, **"Revolution!,"** we shall have a brief closing. It is quite possible that in the future of our days, equality and justice shall demand forceful consideration and heightened participatory action by many to rectify past critical mistakes having been performed on a grand scale. This rectification shall be accomplished in a voluntary and conciliatory manner and hopefully seen as a quiet, **"enlightened revolution."** And if there are those that would wish to pretend to be blind to prior "indiscretions," and continue to demand their high perch on the apex of material greed, be it noted that a revolution will still arise. It will not be calm, quiet, without great pain, or needless suffering – for the world cannot continue to be spinning backwards for billions of its inhabitants while the rest of us stick our heads in the sand and feign ignorance.

Are you a Latino star athlete who thrills fans every day/night with your superior athletic abilities? Did you know that you are still a second-class person in the U.S.A. because, "Your English, she is not so good." Are you a movie star, "famous" person with Latino roots? Perhaps the time is now for all of you to stand up and be counted as supporting your Native countrymen. They desperately need your voice and someone to be an advocate for them. You know of the struggles your people have gone through. You or your family members probably went through the same suffering that most of the poor deal with everyday. Now that you have been graciously blessed, become a true shining star. Roberto Clemente, the great Puerto Rican baseball player died in a plane crash carrying relief supplies to the people of earthquake devastated Managua, Nicaragua in 1972. He was great when I saw him play, but I'll always remember him more for his big, giving heart.

And be creative my friends. Do you know of the restless, active Boy on a Cott with 2 Ts?

~ **The Ballad of No Más** ~   (No More)

No Más will we work for slave wages in your sweat shops.
No Más will we allow you to steal our bountiful resources.

No Más will we allow you to discriminate against us because of the ebony, chocolate, pearl, golden yellow, red hills color of our skin.
No Más will we dream of your "American Dream," that is based on thievery, but we will give birth to dreams that are honest and of our own spirit and imagination.

No Más will you incarcerate our sons and daughters without true cause.
No Más will we let your military men make whores of our young women.
No Más will we let you capture our best minds.
No Más will we allow you to rule over us, beat us.

No Más will we let you tip the balance of **Justice** with your gun barrels.
No Más will you take away my language – kill my past, my culture, My Self.
No Más will you steal the future of our children's dignity and prosperity.

And yes, we may not know much about politics, but this we do know, "**No Más**" shall be the new Revolutionary cry heard around the world from our deep hearts, parched lips, and from those that support us who also believe in the true equality of the family of man.

Part IX.
Short Stories-

1. "Santiago Meets el Siva Negro"

2. "From Manzarosa to Slab City"

"The Visit"- 24' x 36"

1.
"Santiago Meets el Siva Negro"

"El Pato." The Duck. That's what he called himself every time he closed his eyes and imagined swimming back and forth across the Río Bravo, the river called the Great Divide or La División. The flag with an águila, eagle, was on one side, and a flag with 'estripes and lots of 'estars on the other. He had crossed the river that got his back baptized plenty of times with no problema. He did not realize it but eight years ago, before he ever took his first breath, he had become a strong swimmer; first as his father's fast silk worm (his father was from China) and then as his mother's boyfish inside her womb.

Santiago was his name today, though. And he now found himself in a small ranch en Los Estados Unidos, when just yesterday, he was kneeling next to his cardboard bed in Mexico asking God to provide a meal of birotes, hard rolls, for him and his mother. Had God more than answered his small prayer? The cardboard bed hoped so because it was tired of having its edges bitten off by small hungry teeth.

Most of the first day was spent chatting with Pepino, the young boy of the ranch. Pepino was ten, two years older than Santiago. As they talked, they saw a young but old-looking black man limping along the dirt road. Pepino said, "See that old man there? His name is Siva. When I was little and wouldn't go to sleep, Papá would rap on the wooden wall, make a knocking sound with his knuckles. He would then say, "Aquí viene el Siva!" "Here comes Siva!" "Of course I could not sleep after that, but I did close my eyes and kept very quiet. Now whenever I see him I get sleepy. Sometimes I feel I should apologize to him for being afraid of him all these years without any reason."

Santiago put his hand on Pepino's shoulder, admonished him gently, "Maybe you should, maybe it's God telling you to do that." Pepino never did take Santiago's suggestion.

Weeks later, as Santiago was playing alone out in front of the house, he looked down the road full of dust and stones, and saw el Siva Negro coming. He usually came when it was hot, and he had no shadow. Santiago's first reaction was to run to the back, but he saw el Siva Negro swinging the carved stick cane as a baseball bat and then say, "Go, Say Hey! You're spectacular!"

Santiago being a great baseball aficionado, knew who he was yelling about, and asked, "Te gusta Willie Mays?" "You like Willie Mays, Número 24?"

El Siva Negro was startled. He was first going to say, "You like baseball?" but he caught the question before he threw it. He then asked "Hey kid, can you see me? Most folk can't see me. I thought only other Negro peoples could see me."

"Sí, I can see usted. I can also see Jorge mi amigo at school. Jorge is more darker than me. He is like chocolate on black tar. He holds his bat not right. We try to teach him, but he is like a burro."

"Yep, that's my son Jorge. That little pickaninny. His mother is from Guadalajara. He gets the stubbornness, watery back, and handsome looks from her and the blackness from me." When Jorge was born, his grandfather, Carlos Jamaican-wind, a half-half person, held him up and pressed his ear to his chest, as if to hear the flying fish of his own childhood flying past the moonlit canoes. He also wanted to hear what the faraway talking winds were saying in the Valley of the Sacred Waterfalls. When his abuelo heard the mighty swaying of the coconut palms, he said, "Yes, this is the son of my son. I am well pleased. He is all here."

El Siva Negro gave a small sigh and then asked Santiago in Spanish, "¿Cómo te llamas?""What's your name?"

Santiago said his name and added, "Soy de Méjico," and then asked el Siva Negro, "And where is your place from?"

El Siva Negro told him that the life in his blood came from far away, from a lake in Áfrika, just south of Méjico. He said that when he first met his wife on the Mexican border, he was working on the construction of new fences. One night, when he was working very late and just about to drive away, he saw a familia of mojados (wetbacks) with dry backs crossing illegally to the Estados Unidos. As they were crossing through a dry ravine in the country highway nearby, someone saw a car far away and shouted, without really knowing who it was, "La migra!" ("Immigrations!") To someone crossing illegally, it felt like someone yelling "Fire!" in a nursery fall of babies.

El Siva Negro continued his story. "Anyway, the familia runs and the abuelita (grandmother) of the group falls down and is crowned with many 'bullheads', you know, those stickers that get into you and break off. The poor abuelita had a face that looked like many bees had stung her. I took the family and put them in my troque and drove them close to the Greyhound bus station.

There were five mojados, but I only saw the eyes of one. Santiago, are you too young to know what amor is? This young señorita kept telling me "Gracias, gracias, gracias!" but I didn't hear what she said then for

I kept looking at her eyes. They were like dark Moorish eyes that fell to me from clouds of feathery sand. The next day when mi patrón (boss) heard what I had done, he fired me and gave me a going-away-present; he hit me on my lower leg with a club. I limp to this day because of that gift, but it was all worth it. Two years later, here in town, I saw the lady with the oasis fountains in her eyes working as a waitress in a Mexican restaurant, "El Papagayo." Two months later I am married with her. Nine months later after that, we have a cute, but stubborn mulatto mule boy. I see the day when you two will walk a road of sorrow. The sorrow will make you strong if you don't allow it to kill you."

Santiago told el Siva Negro that he and his mother had a similar experience when he had lost his birth certificate. The certificate showed that he was born in the Estados Unidos, and that Leonila Luz from Chihuahua was his mother; thus they could use it as a passport, but without it, they could not go back and forth on the border as they wished. Santiago added that once when they were crossing illegally, they crossed with a bunch of other people. Most had on six layers of clothing, maybe all the clothes they owned; a few had rolled up serapes for blankets. A man by the name of Señor Oveja was leading the group. Some people paid him muchos pesos to lead them safely across the border. He told everyone to stay together, move as if they were a small hill together; that way they would not be easily recognized. Like the abuelita in the other story, Santiago's mother had also fallen and was greeted by hundreds of hungry torito stickers. She looked like she had a beard and needed a shave. Santiago also recalled that when they went to sleep in an acequia (ditch), there were hungry search lights hunting in the fields without tiring; and that when he woke up, a large cow was walking over him, spilling her cud tobacco juices on his face. And since he had an early morning thirst, he decided to have himself a few free sucks of leche. "Oh, yes. When everybody else woke up, Señor Oveja was gone, gone with everyone's money. He turned out to be more of a wolf than a coyote."

Santiago chatted with his new friend for a long time before he heard Doña Lupe, Pepino's mamá calling. He said, "Adiós." And el Siva Negro said, "Hasta luego, but be very careful where you step, and who is watching those steps. Those steps may lead you faraway if you are not careful."

Santiago wondered what el Siva Negro meant by those last words.

Doña Lupe asked Santiago with a broken glass in her voice, "Why were you talking to Siva?"

"Doña Lupe, you can see el Siva Negro, also?" asked Santiago simply. "He thinks that only other Negros can see him. We were just talking about exciting places like Áfrika, where there are elefantes and gorilas, and about Alabama where they have mean, white tigres that roam around like roaring leones with the mark of KKK on their behinds. In Alabama also they have scary white ghosts with shining fire that glows in their eyes. These ghosts hang black people with lassos in the name of El Señor (the Savior). El Siva Negro showed me then that he too can cry the color of Mejicano tears like mine.

He also told me about his nephew from Chí-ca-go that was called Emmet Till. He died in a river where some gringos tried to use him as fish bait. They said that when they accidentally killed him, they were trying to fly him in the water most deep with a heavy electric fan. When his amigos found him, they took him back to Chí-ca-go to his mamá. Doña Lupe, his good one eye was missing and his other one was lost under his blown up skin. He looked liked a large fat catfish with cuts all over and his guts hanging out. His mamá hurt in her large heart muchísimo, but in her red-fire black skin she was more mad than sad. Maybe that was her manera of not dying. She put her fish boy in a plain box for all in their barrio to see. The body rotted; the cats took parts of him home, and las cámeras de telebishun took the rest of him to all the homes of América at six. Then in words she had heard from her Puerto Rican neighbor, she cried muy loud, "No más! No más!" ("No more! No more!") in a shout heard around el mundo.

Doña Lupe, el Siva Negro also told me about his old girlfriend en Monte Gomery. He called her his Rosa Negra. He told me, "Santiago, when you can read good, real good, read this. It will save your soul. He then gave me an old piece of paper that had this writing on it:

LA ROSA NEGRA (for R. Parks)

Fo' years you walks up them steps,
Hun'red thousands of them.

Fo' years you feeds the hungry coin box
With your last food, and gets no thank yous.

Fo' years you walks to the back
And obeys the sign with the spitting arrow.

Fo' years you sees the backs of angry faces
Staring through their straight hair.

Fo' years you walks fo' me.
Fo' me, fo' me.

But now my flower

I can drive this bus,
Fo' you.

Drive it to the land of promise,
Land of freedom, Land of dreams,

And you can sits next to me,
Yes,
Where a queen sits,

The queen of the Rosa Negra.

~~~~~

"La Raku Geisha" 38" H

2.
"From Manzarosa to Slab City"

On the western side of the Triple X Ranch over a long, 3-foot high black lava wall is a large area of one square mile now called Slab City. It was once called Manzarosa (Rose Apple) in the past. According to the history books in school, between 1910 and 1935 Manzarosa was known as a thriving pear and apple center. Besides the pears and apples, in the old days of May, it was rich in the word "ripe." The birds knew this word well as they would descend upon it from miles around. First they would fly in from the north over giant cottonwoods and then swoop down in a frantic delirium. Where to go first? The western side was full of apple trees of every kind known. There were Strawberry apples, little sweet Lady Apples, Delicious, Crabapples, Roman Beauty, and big Arkansas Blacks, besides the usual Wine Saps. On the southern side was a row of black walnuts, hard nuts for birds to crack, but further on, ah, the cherries and the apricots! The mulberries were on the eastern side. There were all kinds imaginable - the big purple ones, red and even sweet white ones to delight any chickadee's little beak. After gorging themselves to such a buffet, what bird did not look like a bloated Christmas tree ornament stained of multicolored fruit juices. And if they were to adhere to the advice of their mothers, of always drinking after a meal, they would have a nice sip of mineral water from the cool streams of the Granite Reef before heading home.

But those were the days before the Great Drought and days of the U.S. Army's ravenous bulldozers. In the cycle of life, every so often come the droughts which are somewhat understandable, but when a village is created for tiny Japanese American orphans by an over-crazed government with an Executive Order 9066 in hand, one has to know the world has indeed turned itself upside down.

In the summer of 1942, the U.S. Army came and took 3-year old Jeanie Shiraki Sakamoto away from her home. Before the soldiers came, Jeanie lived at a Catholic orphanage in the City of Los Ángeles Perdidos. She was the unwanted baby of a single mother and a married gardener. Maryknoll nuns took care of the girl - first brought to them as a 2-pound premature infant, sick with double pneumonia - until she was forced to leave the only home she knew. She was one of 101 Japanese-American orphans and foster children - some as young as 6 months - quietly rounded up by soldiers with bayonets gleaming during World War II. The children, some with as little as one-eighth Japanese ancestry, were sent to a hastily built orphanage at the Manzarosa Interment camp 300 miles east of the City of Los Ángeles Perdidos. Of course the orphanage directors tried to reason with the soldiers, but to no avail. "I am determined that if they have one drop of Japanese blood in them, they must all go to an internment camp," demanded Col. Carl R. Blendetsen, head of the American Gestapo.

The new orphanage at Manzarosa was known as Children's Village. By Thanksgiving Day, 1942, 90 orphans had been evacuated from as far north as Alaska to southern sunny San Diego, and then sent to Manzarosa because they might be a threat to national security. Somebody had to have had a warped imagination to envision inscrutable little spies with cameras in their diapers. The orphans at Children's Village included babies born to schoolgirl mothers at the internment camps.

The Village was made up of three gift-wrapped-in-tarpaper barracks next to the last surviving pear and apple orchard. The buildings were bigger than the other barracks and included a wrap-around porch and a broad lawn where Japanese deer would graze at night. And unlike the rest of Manzarosa, they had running water and toilets; the toilets were also used by the rats for their drinking water. Sometimes they would fall in and create a huge raucous in the middle of the night. The smaller children would always want to keep the rats as pets. So, the older boys built an elaborate hotel cage in the shape of a pagoda for the long-tailed tenants. The cage was made of old wire hangers and reached from the floor to the ceiling. Up high in the cage were swings where the rats could pretend to be Tarzans or circus trapeze artists. The middle section had wonderful flights of zigzagging stairs. On the cage floor was a large wheel which the teen-age boys constructed so the rats could run and run; the turning of the wheel provided an extra bonus in that it helped to power a small battery flashlight that the children used at night after "lights out" to look through newspapers and magazines searching for prospective parents. The young girls would dress the rats in the geisha doll clothes the older women made for them with their old ornate kimono material. What a sight! "Introducing, Madame Rat Tail Butterfly."

Since the orphans had no families, they had to heavily lean on each other and be creative in how to entertain one another r. Some of the boys would play with marbles that they made by polishing agate, turquoise, and silver stones found in the near-by riverbeds. They would rub and rub the stones on the cement floors until they could see the reflection of their little cat-eye faces. They would also carve beautiful wooden boxes to keep their precious treasures in.

Another game which the young boys played, the ones old enough to be out of diapers was "slam and bang." To play this game the boys would have to first beg ("prease, prease") the camp cooks to give them the paper milk bottle caps. The cooks were always happy to save the caps for them, but first, the one who would "'win" them would have to guess the number of rice grains in five-pound sack of uncooked rice. After the victor settled down from winning and the rest of his friends conspired how to detach him from his prize, they would begin their play. Each boy who wanted to play would first throw in one of his "tokens," into a ring. Then in order, according from youngest to oldest, a boy would try to "slam or bam" one of the caps in the ring. If he were to hit it with one of his, he would get to keep that one. If he didn't, then the new token would stay in the ring. Of course, every time that they would throw a new token in, the "slammer" would yell out "bam!" in a most energetic voice. Sometimes the game would become so fast and furious and the little arena sounded like a Chinese New Year's festival of fireworks.

The older children from other barracks would make shadow puppets of dragons and hawks flying on the rafters. The smaller children who slept on metal folding cots would cheer, "Bonsai!" as the shadows fell on them. The girls in order to entertain themselves would sing songs that they had learned in former orphanages, songs like "God Bless America" and "My Country Tis of Thee." After several of these songs had been sung by a choir of 3-4 year olds, the caretakers, the walls, and birds in the orchards could be heard sobbing uncontrollably. Without the wettest tears, heavy hearts are difficult to swallow. (But, oh what would these poor souls have done if they knew what was happening to the "kin-der" on the other side of the world, in the world where German shepherds were the baby-sitters, and ovens called "Angel Makers" burnt day and night to turn gingerbread children's eyes, fingers, hearts, and breaths into ashes upon ashes.)

These were indeed difficult times for the young children in the village, but undoubtedly the hardest part for them came after the war when the government closed the Children's Village in September, 1945. In the early 1950s, Jeanie Shiraki Sakamoto, who was placed with a white foster family, had a difficult time adjusting to her new surroundings. Sometimes she would gather up her few books, clothes, and lacquered chopsticks and stack them on a table on her room. That way, in an emergency, if her life was disrupted again, she could grab them and run. Life was also tough for her at her San Jacinto junior high school where she was subjected to numerous racial slurs and the usual anti-Asian taunting of 'Chi-na-Chi-na-Japonés-Có-me-Caca-Y-No-Me-Des' (China girl, China girl, Japanese girl, eat shit and don't give me any). Who was she anyway? "I wish I were never Japanese," She recalled thinking. "Perhaps, it would have been better to have been born as a cherry blossom."

After the war, some of the barrack buildings were dismantled, others sold to large farm owners so that they could cram in all of their migrant bracero workers. Thus the same buildings felt "at home" in creating their usual spirit of depression and hopelessness. All that was truly left of the Manzarosa Detention Center and the Children's Village, that it housed, were the skeletal remains of the water faucet pipes sticking out by themselves, growing out from the large empty cement slabs. The cracked cement slabs looked like giant stepping stones for the legendary Sash Quash of the area. Lots of the slabs had mementos deeply scratched with rusty nails into their hard surfaces. Most of the oriental graffiti had dates and names, some had stick-figure drawings of children crying in the night, some were of poems with names like "Farewell Manzarosa" and "Snows Falling on Mt. Fuji Cedars." A most memorable writing was "The past is dead if there is no one to remember, Sayonara Manzarosa."

"SLOWLY"

"There are many ways for people to die, but somehow dying of starvation is the most unacceptable of all. It happens in slow motion. Second by second, the distance between life and death becomes smaller and smaller, until the two are in such close proximity that one can hardly tell the difference. Like sleep, death by starvation happens so quietly, so inexorably, one does not even sense it happening. And all for the lack of a handful of rice at each meal. In this world of plenty, a tiny baby, who does not yet understand the mystery of the world, is allowed to cry and cry and finally fall asleep without the milk she desperately needs to survive. The next day she does not have the strength to go on living."

Mohammad Yunus, Nobel Peace Prize Winner 2006
(Bangladesh)

~~~~~~~~~~~~

In the end as in the beginning, the true question still remains in spite of all our nebulous thoughts, speculations- whether unfounded or quite reasonable on both sides of this issue, WWYD? Truly, What Would You Do? What would you do if <u>your</u> children were dying because of the lack of medicine, or starving for the lack of food? Thank you for being the first to have crossed the "illegal" fence to justice. You have finally learned to be "More than an American..." You have become a human being again.

~~~~~~~~~~~~~~~~~~~~~~~~~

Step Outside of Yourself...
Live Beyond the Illusion
And Touch someone's Life
With an open Heart and caring Hands.

~~~~~~~~~~~~~~~~~~~~~~~~~

Author's Note:

By today's political outcry, I guess I would now be considered an "anchor baby" since my mother was illegally from Chihuahua and my father illegally from China. Is that why I became a semi-precious child of a mixed-up God over sixty years ago and now need to be deported?

Profits from the sale of this book (50%) and the author's artwork will be donated to immigrant rights issues and to assist children who wish to leave a World most of us will never know. Salamat.

"<u>More Than An American</u>" can be ordered from: jimlarriva.com

"Market Vendor" 24"x36"

About the author:

Born half Gila monster, half split bamboo,
By light hid in the ashes of the copper Phoenix,
By night died in tears of the laughing chameleon.

Born as a floating dandelion seed, wandered,
Beckoned by the teasing tendrils of the Ocean
Ferns that whispered, "You are Found here."
But Beautiful lies are lies just the same.
In midstream died the death of tears three times
As the joys of the loins were torn, abducted, lost.

Born anew as a drifting snowflake in the Rockies,
Thought to be clean, pure as snowness white
But soon began to melt away tear by tear
By the dry heat of the Cruelty, Heartlessness
Of man upon man that
Brought daily haunting visions of

Bound calloused hands from the South and West -
Crying in the desert with split, bleeding lips
"Por favor, let the winds of Justicia
Blow anew, and Forever more be true."

"Breathe not the tears of laughter
Bought by a stolen overflow of greed."
But "Surrender, sacrifice the tears that were
Broken…From your dying utmost Need."